From the Heart of the People

In memory of
Albert I. Koenigsknecht, M.M.,
Prelate of Juli,

who gave his life for the poor
and so gave it to his God

From the Heart of the People,

The Theology of Gustavo Gutiérrez

Curt Cadorette

MEYER
STONE
BOOKS

Published in the United States by Meyer-Stone Books,
a division of Meyer, Stone, and Company, Inc.,
714 South Humphrey, Oak Park, IL 60304

Cover design: Terry Dugan Design

Manufactured in the United States of America.

92 91 90 89 88   5 4 3 2 1

Library of Congress Cataloging-in-Publication Data

Cadorette, Curt, 1948–
    From the heart of the people : the theology of Gustavo Gutiérrez / Curt Cadorette.
        p.   cm.
    Bibliography: p.
    Includes index.
    ISBN 0-940989-27-1
    ISBN 0-940989-18-2 (pbk.)
    1. Gutiérrez, Gustavo, 1928–   . 2. Liberation theology — History.
3. Catholic Church — Doctrines — History — 20th century. I   Title.
BX4705.G786C33 1988
230'.2'0924 — dc19   87-21775
                                                                         CIP

... we will have an authentic theology of liberation
only when the oppressed themselves can freely raise their voice
and express themselves directly and creatively in society
and in the heart of the People of God,
when they themselves "account for the hope" which they bear,
when they are the protagonists of their own liberation.
For now we must limit ourselves to efforts
which ought to deepen and support that process,
which has barely begun.

— A Theology of Liberation, p. 307

Contents

Acknowledgements

This work represents several years of research, but more importantly, years of human experience that preceded it and gave it a particular shape. Its roots lie in the experience of being born to working-class parents who tried to respond with honesty to the North American world they found themselves in. They put together a mosaic of meaning with the bits and pieces offered them by life. In many ways they resembled the Peruvian people of the *altiplano* with whom I spent eight years of my life and who also helped shape this work. Unrecognized and supposedly unarticulate, my Peruvian friends have provided the poetic resonances and depth that motivated me to write. They are people with a remarkable passion for life. Long before I ever read Gustavo Gutiérrez's theology they taught me what the struggle for liberation really means.

The particular content of this work has been shaped by many other people as well. Among them are Lee Cormie, who so generously analyzed its content as it was written and rewritten more times than I can count or care to remember. Mary Hembrow Snyder scrutinized the text with scholarly insight and patience but most importantly offered wise and warm friendship. Ellen Carey, Sue Grace, Liz Mach, and Tony Medwid put up with my foibles for many months and kept me on a more or less even keel as I worked over the manuscript. To those people and many others, my profound thanks.

Preface

Anyone familiar with Latin American liberation theology has noted that its authors rarely refer to their own lives and histories. This reluctance to explain their own background is partially due to their seeing themselves as part of a collective enterprise in which they act as spokespersons for a community of Christians dedicated to liberative praxis. Nonetheless, this dearth of biographical information can be perplexing since liberation theologians place so much stress on history and social context as determining factors in theology.

Knowing a few details about a theologian as a person can give his or her writing more poignancy than it might otherwise have. The personal history, sights, and sounds that give color and conviction to a theologian's words are often as important as the words themselves. Following that line of thought, I begin with a brief description of my own history and experience in Peru in the hope that readers will better understand the source and motivation behind this work. My interest in Gutiérrez's theology is not the result of mere intellectual curiosity. Rather it flows from a privileged experience of having lived among the men and women who provide the raw material of his theology — the poor and oppressed of Peru.

For nearly eight years I worked in a small Peruvian town called Chucuito. Of the string of towns that surrounds Lake Titicaca, Chucuito is one of the most historic and scenic. It contains the ruins of an Inca temple built in the fifteenth century and two Spanish baroque churches constructed by the Dominicans a hundred years later. Its narrow, ancient streets lie on an incline and offer a spectacular view of the lake whose waters change from an intense blue to an emerald green as the sun passes. The lake stretches into the horizon like a living sheet of colors with a life and rhythms all its own. Pondering its expanse one quickly realizes why the Aymara and Quechua peoples who live around the lake hold it in such reverence. It speaks of the power and transcendence of nature. When night falls the sky becomes a riot of stars. The darkness reveals swirls of constellations that pass through the night in patterns so dense it seems possible to reach up and touch them. The commonplace effects of nature, the cycles of day and night, assume an intensity in Chucuito that inspires awe.

Chucuito is located in the Peruvian *altiplano,* a high, semi-arid plateau in the extreme south of the country bordering Bolivia. Nearly thirteen thousand feet above sea level, the *altiplano* is wedged between two Andean mountain ranges that funnel intense, cold winds through the plains. The lake serves as a buffer that warms the air, provides water for crops, and counteracts the monotony of a rock-strewn, nearly treeless environment. The *altiplano* is a land of contrasts. With the advent of rains in the summer months the land becomes lush and verdant. Once they cease in April the cold and dryness return again and a pervasive tone of grayish-brown dominates the horizon. Exquisite beauty coexists with unrelenting, windy harshness. This enigmatic mix of forces pervades more than the atmosphere. It also affects people's lives.

In the *altiplano* existence is a never-ending challenge. People struggle to extract what a harsh and often capricious land begrudgingly offers. About 90 percent of the population consists of *campesinos* who engage in subsistence agriculture. They grow potatoes and barley, which are stored for consumption during the year. Many families have small herds of sheep or alpaca, which provide wool for clothing and occasional cash when it it is sold to local merchants for export. The animals are shepherded by young children and elderly adults. For *campesinos* family responsibilities in the struggle for survival begin at five years of age and end when life ends. Romantic notions of childhood and the pleasantries of old age are concepts no *campesino* family can afford to entertain.

Campesinos in the *altiplano* generally speak either Aymara or Quechua, Andean languages totally unrelated to Spanish, which is the official language of Peru. They are the descendants of once powerful civilizations disenfranchised by Spanish *conquistadores.* The *altiplano* was one of the first areas subjugated by Pizarro's cohorts as they marched toward the silver mines of Potosí. It became a source of cheap and expendable forced labor used in the mines for Spain's glory at the cost of hundreds of thousands of lives.[1] Despite more than four centuries of cultural and political oppression, however, *campesinos* have retained a spirit of independence. This is due in no small measure to the fact that the Spanish were disinclined to view the people they conquered and brutalized as real human beings. Their language and way of life were considered signs of inferiority, the idiom and culture of a slave class best ignored. Yet because their language and culture persisted, albeit relegated to inferior status, *campesinos* managed to preserve a sense of cultural uniqueness. Like many conquered groups, they retained a subtle pride in themselves as a distinct people, which shielded them from cultural annihilation.

Aymara *campesinos* are generally *minifundistas,* i.e., small landowners whose holdings average about three acres. They normally own a number of plots in several areas, some only one or two furrows in width. Different crops are planted in each section to minimize loss due to flooding, drought, hail, and frost. Centuries of experience have taught *campesinos* to spread and rotate crops as a hedge against the climate. They understand the vagaries of subsistence farming and their ancient but effective agricultural techniques generally provide them with adequate sustenance. The Aymara see themselves as participants in a living natural process. They consider their fields, crops, and animals as fellow beings with an identity and spirit of their own. Each plays a specific role in the reproduction of life. Long before western environmentalists were speaking of "ecosystems," Peruvian *campesinos* understood the concept. It is part of their cultural self-understanding and is constantly ritualized in their religious life.[2]

Although figures are far from precise, the cash earnings of a *campesino* family in the Chucuito area average a hundred dollars per year. This money is used to purchase school supplies for children, pay for medical expenses, and buy sundry items unobtainable through barter. The Aymara are not easy to classify in socio-economic terms. In certain ways they participate in capitalist processes to the extent that they own land and sell what surplus products they produce. At the same time they have a deeply ingrained sense of community, collective work, and ownership of land, which is a legacy of their pre-conquest Andean culture. Roughly half the *campesinos,* however, own no land and work as *colonos*; these tenant farmers cultivate the fields of *mestizo* landlords who form a culturally and economically distinct class. By custom *colonos* retain only a third of the crop they so laboriously produce. They have no claim to the land, and if the crops fail for any reason they run the risk of ruin. When the growing season ends many migrate to the coast to work in sugar cooperatives or mines to provide an economic buffer for their families.

The town proper is the domain of the *mestizos* who speak Spanish and identify with Western culture. Unofficial estimates indicate that they own about 70 percent of the arable land and pasturage, although they constitute less than 10 percent of the population.[3] Their disproportionate control of the land is a relatively recent phenomenon that can be dated to the late nineteenth century when British merchants became interested in Peruvian woolen and agricultural products. An economic system based largely on local interchange and barter was replaced by a cash economy increasingly dependent on foreign markets. Hungry for an opportunity to make money, the *mestizos* began to expropriate lands held by *campesinos,* especially communal properties. This was accomplished by the manipulation of land titles, economic coercion, or sheer force.[4] Nearly every *mestizo* family in Chucuito has a relative who practices law. The landowning class thus controls the judicial system, local government agencies, and police. In short, the law is obedient to their class interests. Chucuito is a town with two types of peoples — the powerful and the disenfranchised.

Except for economic interchange *campesinos* and *mestizos* rarely mix. Each group has its language, social network, and history. Even their religious lives vary. *Campesinos* blend traditional Catholicism with Andean rituals. The earth, or *Pachamama*,[5] is identified with Mary. As the most important spiritual personage she is the source and final resting place of all living things. Each hill also has its resident spirit generally associated with a saint who watches over life within his or her domain. The *mestizos* follow the customs of Spanish Catholicism with its stiff, formal rituals and cult of suffering and death. The religious life of *campesinos* is carried on in fields and hills and follows the cycle of agricultural growth. The *mestizos* worship in the confines of dark baroque churches ornately decorated with gold and silver extracted by forced labor from colonial mines. Chucuito, like Peru itself, is a world of doubles with two economic systems, two cultures, and two histories that refuse to admit the legitimacy of the other. The Andes and "Mother Spain" have yet to be reconciled with each other despite five centuries of forced proximity.

At first glance Chucuito seems to be a rather quiet town. Underneath the surface, however, lies a volcano of social tension. The seeming tranquility is betrayed by a constant and bitter struggle that goes on between two distinct peoples who live in antithetical worlds. To remain on top of the social pyramid *mestizos* continually demonstrate their power by intimidating *campesinos,* who naturally resent their oppressive arrogance. To survive as a distinct culture, Aymara *campesinos,* like many oppressed peasant cultures, have developed complex forms of resistance to the *mestizos'* exploitation and socio-economic hegemony.

The two groups constantly spar with each other. Generally the struggle is subtle, an almost unnoticeable cat and mouse game. At times, however, the tension between the groups leads to violent confrontations. The history of the Peruvian *altiplano* is marked by peasant uprisings that were suppressed with bloody force by the police and military. Not surprisingly, these revolts receive no mention in the annals of official history. The antipathy between the two classes is obvious in the language they use to describe each other. The *mestizos* call themselves *gente decente,* the decent people, as opposed to *campesinos,* whom they refer to as *indios,* a word not to be confused with its English cognate. In Peruvian Spanish *indio* has the same racist connotation as "nigger" in English. Behind their backs *campesinos* call the Spanish-speaking townspeople *mistis.* In Aymara *misti* implies a mongrel breed of animal, half dog and half llama. Neither group is prone to use euphemisms about the other.

As a North American steeped in the myths of a middle-class upbringing with its fixation on conformity and social harmony, I was ill prepared to understand the class and cultural tensions of Chucuito. Naïvely believing in the liberal capitalistic values that had been drummed into my head for the better part of twenty-five years, it was difficult to appreciate how bitter the tensions between *campesinos* and *mestizos* really are. I knew in theory that racism and economic injustice existed, but was unable to appreciate what they meant concretely. I was an outsider with fuzzy, abstract values incapable of interpreting how an oppressive, class-stratified society functioned from the inside. Typically, I believed society was "rational" and people in that society could reason and change their lives for the better. Social problems could be overcome with adequate thought, a bit of decency, and Christian "virtue." Events in Chucuito proved that my perspective was very simplistic.

Slowly but surely I was drawn into the cultural and religious conflict of the town, at first unaware of what was happening. When I arrived in Chucuito in 1974, a new pastor had been named for the town. A linguist by training, he spoke Aymara and tried to incorporate the language and indigenous religious rituals into parish services. Slowly the *campesinos* began to respond positively to his openness towards their way of life despite their wariness of the institutional church with its long history of support for the landowning class. They saw their rituals and beliefs being affirmed in a church where they had all too often been denigrated and condemned.

I learned a rudimentary sort of Aymara, convinced that it could only increase my pastoral effectiveness. I failed to realize, however, that speaking Aymara would be interpreted as an affront to the *mestizos'* power and way of life. According to their sensibilities the clergy should speak only Spanish and support the status quo through our religious office. We were expected to be chaplains to oppressors and not consort with the oppressed, especially in their own language. Our loyalties became suspect because we were hearing a very different description of life not at all consonant with the *mestizos'* interpretation. We had violated a long-standing alliance between the dominant class and church and were perceived as dangers to its hegemony.

What remaining liberal notions I had about society were laid to rest in 1978. In April of that year the pastor and I became involved in a protracted confrontation with the *mestizos*. When the pastor celebrated one of "their" fiesta masses in Aymara, they reacted violently. They were convinced that our growing friendship with *campesinos* and appreciation of their culture had reached dangerous extremes. Ever mindful of their status and skillful defenders of their "rights," they were not about to accept this affront to their power. Two of the more prominent *mestizos* devised a scheme to redress the problem: they hired thieves to rob the parish church.

The robbery had two purposes, the first monetary and the second political. Colonial Peruvian art fetches a high price on the international market and the church in Chucuito had several statues and paintings that dated from the early years of the Spanish Conquest. In the *altiplano,* however, the value of religious art is not measured solely in dollars. The well-being of the local community lies in the hands of the saints whose images are revered in the parish church. By blaming us for the robbery, which they did immediately, the *mestizos* were accusing the pastor and me of threatening the well-being of the town by desecrating its life-sustaining symbols. In this way they hoped to destroy a seemingly dangerous alliance between the local parish and *campesinos*.

Fortunately the *mestizos'* scheme did not work. By sheer luck the thieves were caught several days later while carrying out another robbery. Under questioning they implicated the *mestizos*. Before this happened, however, several people in the town, all *campesinos* and friends of the pastor and me, were put in jail, although it was obvious to everyone that they were in no way involved in the robbery. Two spent more than six months behind bars with no charges ever being brought. The *mestizos* knew that jailing two priests might backfire as overkill, but attacking people close to us was all too easy. Because the landowning class controls the judicial system, the police bring or drop charges according to the orders they receive. Being in jail subjects a *campesino* to far more than incarceration. Peruvian prisons are hell-holes where brutality is a given. Prisoners must provide their own food and even cooking utensils. They fight among themselves for a clean, sheltered place to sleep and must constantly buy off guards who threaten them with torture. Only the strongest can resist the dehumanization Peruvian prisons are designed to produce. I went to the jail several times a week to bring food and money to the two men from Chucuito. While I was there dozens of other prisoners would speak to me through the bars pleading for legal advice, food, and money. Many were emaciated and obviously suffering from tuberculosis. I came back from every visit disgusted and shaken.

After protracted legal battles and angry confrontations too complex to describe, the people in jail were freed and the case eventually settled. The actual thieves were sentenced, although the *mestizos* implicated in the robbery were never indicted despite mention during the trial that they had provided detailed drawings of the church and indicated precisely what objects were to be stolen. In fact the official record of the trial was altered and the names of any landowners from Chucuito deleted. They paid bailiffs to "borrow" written testimony at night. Ever respectful of the court's dignity, however, they promptly returned the record in the morning minus names and even pages of evidence. Eventually the entire legal brief "disappeared."

This entire experience proved highly educational. My idealism and simplistic beliefs about society were waylaid by a type of corruption and violence I had never experienced before. I was exposed to a raw, nearly limitless type of power capable of destroying people through lies and intimidation. Most disconcerting for me was the realization that violence was an inherent part of society in the *altiplano,* something people lived with constantly. Under the surface of daily existence was a sophisticated system of oppression. Initially I was also shocked by the seeming passivity of many *campesinos*. Unaware of what centuries of oppression do to a people's will, I could not understand why they appeared to tolerate such patent injustice. It eventually dawned on me that they have practically no legal way of redressing the exploitation they are subjected to, despite a supposedly enlightened legal code that, in theory, respects their equality and way of life.

What I failed to realize at first was that exploitation and violence were subtly woven into the fabric of society and that extricating them required more than idealism. Nor, for that matter, was I subject to their effects as a *campesino* was. As a member of the church and a foreigner I had a great deal of immunity and far less at stake than people who live from crop to crop and are subjected to constant political oppression. Like any foreigner, I might be expelled from the country, but there was little likelihood of going to jail and none of starving to death. My liberal social values were clearly of little use for interpreting the situation and may have been an impediment. It was only when I was exposed to the quiet but violent struggles between the *mestizos* and *campesinos* that it became clear to me that I was in the middle of a class conflict whose outcome profoundly affected peoples' lives. Neutrality in this struggle became impossible.

Taking a stance, however, required that I develop a more realistic understanding of Peruvian society. I needed what Juan Luis Segundo calls a "hermeneutic of suspicion,"[6] which would challenge my simplistic social and religious values. One of the advantages of working in Peru was that it exposed me to committed Christians who were also confronted with complex social questions that challenged their social values and faith; one of the most notable of these being Gustavo Gutiérrez. In my early efforts to understand Peruvian society more adequately I turned to his writings. They struck me as remarkably incisive and comprehensible, a Peruvian theologian's reflections on his own country that used social scientific analysis and reflected a deep Christian commitment to his own people's liberation.

In the pages that follow I will examine Gutiérrez's theology by looking at the world he inhabits. There is a direct connection between the oppression and poverty, vitality and hope of his own people and the theology he has so skillfully crafted in the last two decades. His words flow from his social context and without understanding the latter the former can easily be misunderstood. It is unfortunate that so much of the controversy about liberation theology is the result of ignorance. If its critics spent time with the poor and oppressed instead of speaking about them abstractly, it is likely that they would be more sympathetic. They often fail to realize that the real subjects of liberation theology are Christians committed to the integral liberation of their societies, beset by oppression and sin. Their words are the foundation of Gustavo Gutiérrez's writings. His theology is an expression of their lives as a believing people.

I begin in the only logical place to initiate an analysis of Gutiérrez's theology — in the world of the poor and oppressed. It may seem strange to start a theological study by examining the socio-political and cultural re-

xviii   *Preface*

ality of the Peruvian people, but this is the only valid starting point given the people-oriented theology Gustavo Gutiérrez offers us. After looking at the contours of his world I will examine some of the more important intellectual and literary influences in his writings. Well versed in a number of fields, he draws from a vast array of novelists, social scientists, and philosophers to give realism and flavor to his theology. This will provide an opportunity to study his socio-political sensibilities and, I hope, dispel some of the simplistic notions ill-informed critics entertain about his understanding and use of Marxist social theory. Finally, I will examine some of the key theological themes in his writings, especially his understanding of the person of Jesus and the role of the church in liberative praxis.

NOTES

1. One of the most thorough and scholarly studies of the mining system of colonial Peru is Lewis Hanke's classic work *The Imperial City of Potosí* (The Hague: Nijhoff, 1956).
2. An unrivaled description of the Aymara religious world can be found in Jacques Monast's study *On les croyait chrétiens: les aymaras* (Paris: Les Editions du Cerf, 1969). Also, Michael Taussig's treatment of the socio-cultural world of indigenous Andean peoples provides useful analysis, particularly chapters eight through fourteen. See *The Devil and Commodity Fetishism in South America* (Chapel Hill: University of North Carolina Press, 1980). Taussig is an anthropologist who works from a critical Marxist perspective.
3. Because census figures in Peru do not take social class into consideration, one can only estimate the actual landholdings of the *mestizos*.
4. An insightful study into this historical process can be found in Florencia E. Mallon, "Murder in the Andes: Patrons, Clients, and the Impact of Foreign Capital, 1860–1922," *Radical History Review* 35: 79–98.
5. Pachamama is both an Aymara and Quechua word that means "the mother of all." It is the key religious concept among Andean peoples.
6. See Juan Luis Segundo, *The Liberation of Theology,* trans. John Drury (Maryknoll, N.Y.: Orbis Books, 1976), pp. 7–38, for an explanation of this important concept.

Chapter 1

The Socio-Economic Context

> We have learned to see the great events of the history of the world
> from beneath — from the viewpoint of the useless, the suspect, the
> abused, the powerless, the oppressed, the despised. In a word, from
> the viewpoint of the suffering.   — *Dietrich Bonhoeffer*

These words of Dietrich Bonhoeffer written more than forty years ago have
had a tremendous impact on Gustavo Gutiérrez as a human being and
theologian.[1] He has lived them out in his pastoral work among the people
of his own country and quoted and paraphrased them in various ways in
his writings. They contain a notion basic to his action and thought —
remaking the world in a new and revolutionary way from the viewpoint of
people whose lives and opinions have little if any weight in the oppressive
reality of Latin America today.

In the pages that follow we shall examine how Gutiérrez responds to
Bonhoeffer's challenge to remake society and history from the bottom up,
from the viewpoint of the "powerless" and "despised." To do this, however, requires some familiarity with Peru and its people, the majority of
whom are desperately poor by First World standards. That task is not
easy despite the romantic and ultimately ideological notion many entertain about the "simplicity" of the oppressed. They are complex human
beings whose lives are not easily described by words nor adequately represented by statistics. The world of the poor is a complicated microcosm
only dimly appreciated by outside observers who all too often are blinded
to what they see by their own class and educational backgrounds.

The poor respond to oppression in complex ways, some surviving and
others perishing for reasons that often defy adequate description. Socially
marginalized and exploited, they suffer intense pain and yet continue to
hope. They have their own culture, language, and religion with which
they express their deepest human feelings in poignant and yet complicated
ways. Entering the world of Peru's poor can be an uncomfortable, even
threatening experience for those of us accustomed to discreet and ordered

analysis. Poverty and oppression are forces that rip at a person's body and soul leaving little room for abstraction or dispassionate discourse. But as Gutiérrez has pointed out, this is the only valid place in which theology can be done in a world marked by massive oppression and suffering.[2]

Like few other theologians, Gutiérrez is deeply sensitive to the oppression and hope of the poor with whom he lives and from whom he comes. He knows the meaning of struggle because, like so many other Peruvians, struggle has been a part of his life. He grew up in a loving family, but one of very limited economic means. His father was a poor urban worker and his mother unschooled. As a child he spent several years bed-ridden with osteomyelitis, which left him lame. Gifted with an acute intelligence, he managed to excel academically despite his physical handicap.[3] Certainly he could have used his talents to move up the socio-economic ladder, but chose not to. He first studied medicine at the national university of San Marcos in Lima, but later switched to the diocesan seminary because he thought the priesthood afforded a more direct way to address the needs of the poor.

The world Gutiérrez inhabits is one of dialectical extremes with few buffers between. Death and life, oppression and liberation, exploitation and freedom are very real forces in the lives of ordinary Peruvians. They are not abstract concepts as they are for many people from middle-class, capitalist societies who have been anesthetized by religion and ideological education to the oppression and pain their socio-economic system unleashes in the world around them. Most Peruvians are the victims of capitalism, not its beneficiaries. They are underpaid, undernourished, deprived of satisfaction in life, and often brutally repressed when they challenge the prevailing order. Yet they tenaciously fight for a better life, if not for themselves then for their children.

This experience of suffering and hope is a constant theme in Gutiérrez's writings, and he employs various terms to analyze its complex workings. In theological language he often describes the struggle affecting the poor as a contest between sin and salvation. In political and sociological terms he often uses concepts like ideology and utopia to explain the dialectical events that transpire in Peruvian society. This type of language runs throughout Gutiérrez's works, but it is not indicative of simplistic social analysis or theological dualism. His writings reveal an awareness of the complex interplay between the forces of oppression and liberation. Furthermore, he uses the insights of other theologians and social scientists to give added depth to his own ideas.

When Gutiérrez discusses any theological or social concept, be it sin, salvation, ideological oppression, or the utopic vision of the poor, his ultimate interest is to discover what the term means among his own people. He is not concerned with theoretical definitions per se, but rather with understanding how such concepts unlock the deeper significance of oppressed peoples' lives. In Third World countries like Peru social sin translates into exploitation, physical pain, and premature death for millions of people. Likewise, the hope of the poor evident in their struggle for survival makes life possible despite nearly genocidal exploitation.

To say that sin destroys life while hope saves it is not to engage in metaphorical language but to state a palpable fact. The social and theological, theoretical and concrete are accordingly linked together in the life of the poor and in Gutiérrez's theology. His is not a world of distinct planes that separate our mental and spiritual activities from our social and physical existence. Rather they blend together. This explains why Gutiérrez's theology is ultimately so practical. It speaks of and to the lives of the poor. In the final analysis his writings are their self-perception and expression as people of faith.

Without a sense of the human characteristics and dynamism of Gutiérrez's world, our discussion runs the risk of sinking into abstraction. To some degree at least we must feel what it is like to live with daily exploitation, with inadequate wages if any, with the knowledge that achieving a better life is nearly impossible and that a person's only hope often lies in a distant future embodied in her or his children. This is a world few North Americans or Europeans experience, but it is the daily fare of the millions of Third World men and women who are the overwhelming majority of this planet's inhabitants.

Third World Capitalism: The Seamy Side of "Progress"

I consider contemporary Peruvian society to be a society marked by a capitalist mode of production which oppresses and robs ordinary people. The system in which we live, the social, economic and political system, is the cause of this situation of injustice, poverty, and marginalization. This fact has been clearly pointed out in Medellín and Puebla. For this reason I want and try to struggle for a society built in terms of the interests and aspirations of the poor....I would say that this is my general posture in terms of the country. I also believe it is my way of being faithful to the Gospel.[4]

As the citation above makes clear, Gutiérrez holds straightforward opinions about the way Peruvian society operates and the challenges it presents to him as a Christian and theologian. His negative assessment of capitalism is a result of thorough study of how this system has worked in the past and continues to operate in most Latin American countries. As we shall see, Gutiérrez has more than an amateur's grasp of socio-economic theory. But his rejection of capitalism is as much the result of his living with its human costs as it is of theoretical analysis.

Gutiérrez lives and works in Rimac, one of Lima's oldest *barriadas,* or working-class districts. There one sees endless *tugurios,* rows of cell-like, single rooms sometimes inhabited by whole families. Few have running water or even more than one bed. Although nearly 60 percent of the population has no stable employment, some of the inhabitants have jobs in nearby factories working for transnational corporations such as Bayer Chemical or B. F. Goodrich. After ninety days those who labor in these factories are often routinely fired. Employers are not required by law to pay social security, health insurance, or retirement benefits to workers employed less than three months. If the economy allows it, some people may be eventually rehired if, of course, they have not engaged in union work or left-wing political activity. Employers keep a close watch on their workers, enticing some to spy on others with promises of increased wages and job stability. If rehired they can expect to make about three dollars a day until the next layoffs are announced.

Working conditions are often dangerous and industrial accidents frequent. If injured, workers are simply laid off and employers have no legal obligation to compensate them. Although the factories are financially lucrative, they are in a process of permanent deterioration because plant operators refuse to reinvest their profits in machinery and physical structures. Despite the hazards and exploitation they experience, however, most workers consider themselves exceedingly lucky. Unlike most of their neighbors, they have a modest income. As Gutiérrez knows, Rimac is a place where people experience hopelessness and children often die of tuberculosis before five years of age. Here the immorality of Third World capitalism is not open to debate. It can be seen, heard, and touched.

To quote a common refrain, Latin America is a continent where the "poor are getting poorer and the rich are getting richer." In the more sophisticated language of John Paul II, it is a continent where "the growing affluence of a few people parallels the growing poverty of the masses."[5] John Paul goes on to note that the poverty of millions in Latin America is systemic, that is, it is the result of the way society is currently structured and not the result of ill fate

Gutiérrez cites the pope because his words explain the root cause of poverty and exploitation in so many Third World countries. What John Paul II says clearly is that poverty is the result of distorted human values, values that allow one person to exploit another in the name of power and gain. In conventional theological language poverty is primarily a result of sin. Its origin lies in a refusal to accept one's brothers and sisters as real human beings and co-heirs in God's gift of creation. This refusal is translated into dehumanizing political structures that sap the labor and dignity of millions of Third World peoples.

One need only spend a day in Lima to realize that there is something awry in Peruvian society. A few kilometers from Rimac lies Monterico — literally "Rich Hill," where swimming pools are considered essential for dignified living. Yet in many *pueblos jovenes* dozens of families share one spigot, if there is water at all. These extremes of poverty and wealth are directly related. As Gutiérrez notes, the discrepancy between Peruvian elites and the impoverished masses also has an international parallel evident in the socio-economic differences between developed and so-called underdeveloped nations. Peru is merely a reflection of a much larger problem.

The distance between the poor countries and the rich ones in our capitalist world is widening, as numerous studies by international agencies have shown. The upsurge of capitalism, and the situation of the poor, in recent decades has demonstrated once again that capitalist development is of its very nature detrimental to the masses, as the naked exploitation now endured by the poor nations of the world all too abundantly attests.[6]

The majority of Peruvians with jobs work for economic interests they neither control nor truly benefit from. Peruvian workers produce a wide array of goods — for North America, Europe, and Japan. Peru is burdened with immense debts, owed primarily to American banks. Between 1980 and 1985 nearly 70 percent of the country's export earnings was used to pay interest on loans.[7] This explains why Peruvians are now poorer than ever and increasingly frustrated as they see the work of their own hands slip out of their reach. The fabric of society has been worn thin by the abrasion of poverty that threatens to undo the country.

According to Portes and Walton, two economists whose ideas closely resemble those of Gutiérrez, we are now confronted with an "integral world-system"[8] capable of ever more efficient, integrated, and international economic exploitation. Despite regional variations, the pattern in Latin America is generally the same. The "integral world-system" is pauperizing people. Jobs are disappearing, inflation is rampant, and national indebtedness is out of control. Furthermore, there is a correlation between the power of international capital and the prevalence of right-wing, repressive governments. Caught in a vicious circle of indebtedness and loan "rollovers," political leaders have increasingly resorted to repressive tactics to extract greater labor from the population at large. Yet the economic system responsible for the misery of millions is touted by national elites and international agencies, particularly those connected with the United States government, as the salvation of the poor. As Portes and Walton point out, we are dealing with a value system or ideology that transcends national borders.

As with capital and labor, the circulation of ideas has become accelerated and extended with the expansion of the world-system. This has brought about a growing, although seldom noted convergence in the ideological notions legitimizing inequality in both center and periphery.[9]

Thus one can hear the virtues of capitalism extolled in the government-controlled media of Lima, Santiago, or Washington with the same rhythm and tone. The poor who bear the burden of exploitation and long for a more just social system, however, often suffer in anonymity. As Gutiérrez notes in words reminiscent of Isaiah, "the vast Latin American majorities are dispossessed and therefore compelled to live as strangers in their own land."[10] Deprived of the fruit of their own labor, the poor are victimized by a socio-economic system that shackles them to ever increasing deprivation, despite its rhetoric of advancement and freedom.

As economists have pointed out, during the past two decades the power of the capitalist system has increased enormously in Latin America due to the presence of multinational corporations. They have developed efficient techniques for extracting natural resources and labor power from one country and transferring them to another with little regard for frontiers. In *The Power of the Poor in History,* Gutiérrez explains what the growth of multinationals has meant concretely for the oppressed:

> During these years of the "big boom" of international capitalism, the proliferation of the transnationals gave rise to an ever more important trade network among them, but of such a nature that the term "trade" is used in a very attenuated sense: it should imply a minimum of autonomy on the part of the contractual parties. In fact, however, the assigned cost and market value of a product floated free of its real cost and value, and world capital became extremely liquid. Now the methods of "decapitalizing" the poor countries became even more sophisticated, and their effectiveness in exploiting labor and producing hunger was greatly improved.[11]

As Gutiérrez makes clear, "decapitalizing" a country is not merely an abstract economic process that concerns only bankers. It entails paying workers lower wages while charging them higher prices for basic commodities. It means pillaging a country's natural resources with no regard for its inhabitants or future. It is an unethical, consciously planned process that dehumanizes and kills millions of people. As Gutiérrez points out, the victims of the dominant system are in a "no-win" situation:

> The outlook for the poor is dismal, then, whether the capitalist system prospers or languishes. In either case the function of underdeveloped economies is to provide more capital, either to enhance an already flourishing foreign economy or to collaborate in the solution of its problems.[12]

The only people in a "winning" position are the national elites and members of multinational corporations whose incomes increase while those of workers decrease.

Capitalism in Latin America is more than a mere mode of economic exchange. It is a total socio-economic system that shapes the way people understand and relate to their national state. Rather than being an expression of collective will and vision, the state functions in many Latin American countries as a social mechanism utilized by the politically empowered sector to further its own class-related aims. Local elites who are allied with the interests of international capital control the state in a manner that is best described by the Spanish term *anti-popular,* that is, in ways detrimental to the interests of the majority. As the noted Latin American economists Cardoso and Faletto point out, they facilitate the "penetration of multinationals" among their own people, thus "furnishing the multinationals with the resources for accumulation"[13] extracted from their own countries. The tragic outcome of this process of decapitalization is that the state is converted into an organ of exploitation whose finality is to guarantee the smooth operation of a classist economic system.

As Gutiérrez indicates, the rise of national security states in Latin America is not difficult to explain. They are a result of capitalism's insatiable need for surplus labor and the willingness of national elites to exploit their own people in its acquisition. Looking for ever more efficient means to generate wealth, the dominant economic sector and military have attempted to turn their countries into disciplined camps where defending the status quo is the order of the day and questioning the norms of international capital is deemed treason.

> We shall have to come to appreciate the inadequacy of talk about "the state." The state does not parachute in from another planet. We must take account of the economic and social interests lying behind political power. For example, if we fail to grasp the role of the multinational corporations and the current structure of international capitalism, we shall scarcely be in a position to understand the political systems that have implanted themselves in Latin America in response to popular movements during recent years.[14]

Touted as a bulwark against Marxism and anarchy the national security state functions, in fact, to guarantee the reproduction of the status quo. A mix of repression and immense amounts of nationalistic propaganda are employed to dull the consciousness of workers to their pain and exploitation.

In many Latin American countries the military sees its primary role as defending the country against the internal "threat" of an articulate and organized working class.[15] Thus military experts in "counter-insurgency" strive to coopt and neutralize the people they perceive to be the greatest threat to national stability: the poor. Labor leaders, uncooperative politicians, and members of basic Christian communities are branded as enemies of the state that must be controlled and, if control proves impossible, "liquidated." If this seems like hyperbole, then one need only study the types of people made to "disappear" in so many Latin American countries.

The advent of multinationals and national security regimes in Latin America has resulted in a tragic socio-political schizophrenia. An immense gap has been breached between the ideals of democratic liberalism enshrined in the constitution of Latin American states and the actual sociological role of government. As Cardoso and Faletto indicate, there is a wide discrepancy between the promises of capitalist states to better people's lives and the actual experience ordinary people have of its effects.

> In general, distant goals for the welfare of all are proposed, and in the meantime, not only the freedom but also the material well-being of the national majority is sacrificed, in spite of economic performances that are impressive for those who benefit from them.[16]

This situation points to the fact that capitalism, as it is currently understood and practiced in Latin America, is generating a crisis of political self-understanding. The way the rich and poor perceive and respond to the state is becoming increasingly distinct. The former use it to further their own ends while the latter are its victims. To some degree the discrepancy is covered over by nationalistic propaganda whose purpose is to obfuscate the discrepancy between political ideals and the daily oppression of ordinary people, thus maintaining some type of social cohesion between classes. Nonetheless, feelings of frustration and anger among the poor cannot be entirely repressed. Even the most ingenious propaganda cannot hide the fact that the poor are poorer and the rich richer.

These observations can be made more comprehensible by examining how the discrepancy between the ideal and real is played out in the lives of Peru's urban poor. Sociologists estimate that between two and five thousand people arrive in Lima in any given week in search of work. These immigrants pour into the city from the *sierra* and *altiplano* hoping to support themselves and their families. Lima is the promised land of Peru's poor. However, since only 37 percent of the adult population has stable employment, the chances of finding a job are slim. Even if some do find work wages are so minimal that most migrants to Lima will only exchange the misery of the *campo* for the poverty of an urban slum.

Lima is a city of frustrated hopes where lives are cheapened by a socioeconomic system that regards people as expendable commodities or, in Gutiérrez's term, "non-persons."[17] This experience generates a distinct range of reactions. Some people become demoralized and fatalistic. Others are consumed with frustration and anger that extremist groups like *Sendero Luminoso*[18] adeptly capitalize on. Fortunately, however, a certain percentage of the poor become increasingly self-conscious and politically aware. It is this segment of the poor that resists the demoralizing effects of enforced poverty and begins to challenge the status quo.

It becomes obvious when we look at the socio-economic life of Latin

American countries that a number of antithetical forces are at work. As the consciousness of certain members of the oppressed sector increases so does the reach and power of international capital. Both the poor and the rich are caught in an intricate web of events that even the most astute analysts struggle to understand. A good example of the complexity of things is the international debt crisis that so profoundly affects Peru and other Third World nations. The world's financial system is now so interconnected that Latin Americans pay billions of dollars more in debt payments when the American prime rate increases one percentage point. In an article in *Quehacer* analyzing Latin America's indebtedness, the Peruvian economist David Tejada analyzes how the system works in concrete financial terms:

> Given the structure of payments for 1984, it can be calculated that each percentage point of increase in interest rates, i.e., the prime U.S. and London rates, obliges the Latin American countries to pay an additional sum of $2,500,000,000. In the last few months the rates of interest in the United States have increased more than 2 percent.[19]

These figures undoubtedly require adjustment at the present moment, but clearly indebtedness is more than an economic problem. Paying several billion dollars in interest wreaks havoc with the social fabric of Latin American countries. Poverty and suffering increase in response to monetary obligations imposed by affluent First World nations. We are confronted with a destructive, unpredictable system whose cost to the majority of people in this world is humanly unbearable, not to mention anti-evangelical.

Given the profit-oriented values and policies of international capitalism, it is not surprising that economic disparity, dehumanization, and violent reaction characterize the social climate of many Third World countries. Those at the "top" of the social pyramid no longer view the poor as citizens with rights or even as human beings who merit ethical treatment. When textiles can be produced more cheaply in Lima than in North America, industrialists and banks set up the necessary factories. If economic conditions change or profitability decreases, workers are simply fired, plants closed, and operations transferred to a more profitable country. Profit, not human development, is the "bottom line" for international capital. As Portes and Walton indicate, the market "requirements of global accumulation have redefined Latin America away from its traditional role as a market and, increasingly, into that of a source of cheap industrial labor."[20] Tragically, that labor is provided by a vast army of nameless "non-persons" whose lives are "cheapened" as well.

As Cardoso and Faletto mention, even the hopes and aspirations of ordinary people are now branded as political threats to the ruling faction since "all that is authentically popular, even if lacking the character of specific class demands, has come under suspicion, is considered subversive, and encounters a repressive response."[21] People who speak of hope and work for a just society are treated as enemies of the state by those who monopolize its power for their own ends. In the name of human development and even "Christian civilization," international capitalism and national security states have disenfranchised and oppressed the very people they claim to be assisting.

In Gutiérrez's opinion, reforming the present socio-economic system in Latin America is impossible. The power of the dominant sector is such that it tries to undo any effort at reform. As we shall see, during the late 1960s a moderate military government in Peru attempted to readjust the national economy in a slightly more equitable way. Infused with liberal idealism, a group of progressive generals attempted to create a type of state capitalism that would obviate the worst abuses of the prevailing system. Their efforts quickly met resistance. Peru was branded a "socialist" state by the foreign press. The national oligarchy managed to sabotage almost all the reforms the government implemented in a series of protracted social battles. The so-called Peruvian Experiment, which many hailed as the advent of a new socio-economic model that would diminish class division and create a sense of national purpose, was ultimately a disaster. Gutiérrez makes clear reference to what happened in his own country in *The Power of the Poor in History:*

> The possibility of significantly improving the distribution of income by correcting some aspects of the system's functioning, without altering the system itself, is no longer believable after the experience of many attempts at "reform" in Latin America. These experiences clearly demonstrate that those with capital are not willing to accept redistribution of income, and that the most trifling attempts to better the situation of the majority of the people will be met without fail, in most countries, by the removal of capital, business boycotts, disinvestment, promotion of black markets, and political sabotage. It is clear that international capital seeks countries that offer submissiveness and cheap labor, and that when it does not find those conditions in one country it goes elsewhere in search of better conditions for exploitation.[22]

Gutiérrez's own experience has taught him that the present system cannot be reformed because those who hold power will not permit it. They will not practice justice because their self-serving ideology absolves them from any responsibility toward others except for occasional charity. They are convinced that poverty is not their fault. They may sometimes respond altruistically to the poor, but not as human beings with a right to organize society in a more just, classless way.

So far we have been analyzing the socio-economic characteristics of Peru and Latin America in general terms. To concretize the discussion I will examine the last thirty years of Peruvian socio-economic history in greater detail. In many ways Peru provides a classic case of a Third World country seeking a model for development and finding unexpected success and failure along the way. It is also along this often arduous route that Gutiérrez has come to understand the relationship between social life, committed belief, and the deeper theological meaning of liberation in an oppressive world.

Case Study: Peru 1950–1984

In the early 1950s the Peruvian oligarchy set in motion a process of economic change that would profoundly alter the country's social fabric. Since the sixteenth century Peru had been a supplier of agricultural produce, such as sugar and cotton, and of precious metals. The moneyed class served as intermediaries and managers in a process of natural resource extraction. The vast majority of the working population was involved in a semi-feudal agricultural system or in labor-intensive mining. All this began to change when the dominant sector initiated a process of industrialization and modernization after the Second World War. They used their capital to create factories, primarily in Lima and Arequipa, where textiles and other products made from Peruvian raw materials could be manufactured and sold on the international market.

Their motives were both monetary and, to some degree, altruistic. They clearly stood to make greater profits as entrepreneurs of finished goods than as exporters of raw materials. Furthermore, in accord with the logic of liberal capitalism, they believed national wealth would "trickle down" to the lower echelon of society. Ultimately this process would result in a more unified, progressive society that could stand on its own economic feet. Former peasants were lured to Lima by promises of real wages and the opportunity to break out of the feudal "backwardness" they had experienced for countless generations. Industrialization and urbanization went hand in hand. In addition, this process was meant to defuse the growing threat of radicalization among the poor. Shocked by events in Cuba and confronted with a Marxist-oriented guerrilla movement in the Cusco area, the oligarchy felt that promises of economic reform and social betterment could minimize growing resistance to its hegemony. Industrialization was the great panacea promised to all as a solution for the nation's problems.

The "readjustment" of the economy received a boost in the late sixties when a military government under Juan Velasco took over Peru. Surrounded by a new breed of military technicians who had studied economics and political science in foreign universities and military academies, Velasco set out to make Peru a model of efficient state capitalism and lay the foundation for a new society founded on a well established middle class.[23] Initially, the military met with success. Production and wages rose. Despite the suppression of unions, the military government had wide support and went to great lengths to demonstrate its "populist" character.

Great effort was expended cultivating the political loyalties of the working sector. Schools and clinics were set up in Lima's slums to prove that the quality of life was improving and wealth was indeed trickling down to ordinary people. A propaganda agency was established to disseminate the government's philosophy of development. It controlled the press, radio, and television, reshaped school curricula, and even tried to coopt the Catholic Church into accepting its line of thought. In 1969 the Social Action Committee of the Bishops' Conference actually published a document entitled *La justicia en el mundo,* which advocated a type of democratic socialism as the most promising and ethical socio-political system for Peru.

The seeds of a potential disaster, however, were being sown unbeknown to most people. The government was spending billions of dollars on arms and ill-advised industrial mega-projects convinced they would facilitate "modernization." In fact, the government was almost hounded to borrow by banking consortiums trying to dump excess petrodollars. In 1973 alone over six billion dollars were borrowed for nearly eighty projects. The interest rates, however, seemed reasonable and optimism reigned in the country as significant industrialization took place.

This situation changed quickly with the 1973–1977 world recession. The price of minerals, a Peruvian staple export, dropped precipitously. Many of the mega-projects were hopelessly snarled and draining the treasury. The only way to pay back loans was to turn to the International Monetary Fund. A familiar Third World scenario was set in motion. The I.M.F. consolidated Peru's debts on the condition that the country's economy be restructured in a more "efficient" way. Multinationals whose activity had been restricted during a process of limited nationalization under the military were given free reign once again. The national currency was made to float on the international market. Natural resources were priced in accord with "true" market value as determined in New York. The government allowed open importation of food and medicines and discontinued subsidizing them. Government spending for education and health expenses was cut drastically. The right to strike was curtailed and union activity restricted more than ever.

Desperate for income, the government decreased workers' wages to increase its export earnings. Between 1977 and 1979 wages fell nearly 30 percent and still continue to decline. Peru reached a point where its economy was geared primarily toward debt payment rather than its own citizens' needs. Paying the debt produced socio-economic chaos. By 1983 inflation had reached 125 percent while per capita production dropped more than 15 percent. Peru suffered the unenviable fate of being considered a high risk economic "basket case" by international banks.

We must keep in mind that the people who pay back Peru's debt are the poor themselves. Thomas Burns provides a poignant analysis of what the current economic crisis meant for a typical Peruvian family in 1984:

What does all this mean concretely? It means that the average worker who was the main source of sustenance for 6 people in 1973 is now the principal breadwinner for 8 people with 60 percent less income. It means that if the average worker were to buy two very large loaves of bread (they don't) and pay his or her busfare back and forth to work each day, there would be no money left over at the end of the month. To feed four people a nutrition-poor diet for one month would cost $65; 80 percent (employed or underemployed) of the people earn the minimum wage or less ($50) and the "workforce" is comprised of only 30 percent of the population.

Obviously the implications in terms of diet, morbidity and mortality rates are tragic beyond the telling. Over 50 percent of those who die in Peru are under 5 years of age. And yet the government has reduced its health budget from 4.6 percent of the national budget in 1982 to 3.8 percent in 1984. (In 1968 it was 17 percent).[24]

Gutiérrez sees the human face of these statistics every day. Calling it a "situation of sin"[25] as he does is the result of honest observation as well as moral outrage. What is especially ironic about this tragedy is that Peru has large crude oil reserves, vast deposits of copper and iron ore, and the means to be agriculturally self-sufficient. Somewhat sarcastically, Peruvians refer to themselves as *mendigos sentados en una banca de oro,* beggars sitting on a golden pew. Why, then, is such a naturally rich country so impoverished? Why do people suffer the afflictions of poverty when they should enjoy the benefits of their country's natural wealth?

The Origins of the Crisis: Capitalism and Ideology

In Gutiérrez's opinion the socio-economic oppression Peruvians experience is not simply the result of economic vagaries or miscalculations made by the ministry of finance. The present crisis is rather an inevitable outcome of the way capitalism functions as a socio-economic system. Looking over the economic and political history of Western society in the past several centuries, Gutiérrez sees a complex web of events that helps explain why so many people have been and are impoverished. The expansion of Western society is quite clearly bound up with the development of capitalism, and it is primarily the contradictions of this cultural and socio-economic system that explain the suffering of the poor, past and present.

The proponents of capitalism have been quick to describe this system as the most just and free, the most humane and challenging, but when one looks at the balance sheet these claims are dubious. Rhetoric aside, one of the most striking characteristics of capitalism is that it violates the very principles it claims to defend. For example, the virtues of freedom and self-determination that have been proclaimed as fundamental social principles since the Enlightenment and French Revolution were contradicted by the effects of commodity exchange and the inhuman reification of labor so characteristic of nineteenth-century society. The upper and middle classes advocated freedom but actually disallowed it by the very rules of exchange that undergirded their power. Concepts like freedom and self-determination were and are recast as ideological props that allow destructive competition and class stratification in the name of progress.[26] Semantically speaking, virtues were distorted into vices. This same process of double-talk goes on today.

For Gutiérrez capitalism's contradictions are epitomized in the ethos of bourgeois culture that has dominated Western society since the Enlightenment. Predicated on seeming refinement and an abstract morality, this particular cultural expression of capitalism lived off ruthless oppression of working people who were deemed less than human and therefore freely victimized with no moral compunction. Thus the social class that so loudly proclaimed the new found freedoms of the Enlightenment and French Revolution actually betrayed them in practice. Class interest and personal gain were the real "moral" principles of bourgeois society. The appalling working conditions of most nineteenth-century laborers prove the point.

Nonetheless, Gutiérrez recognizes that without the bourgeoisie the Enlightenment and French Revolution would never have gotten off the ground. With its aristocracy decayed and demoralized, Europe's middle classes took the intellectual and political initiative. They were learning something of crucial importance — that people can shape history according to their will and needs.

> The eighteenth century marks the beginning of revolution in different fields of human activity. In this period, humanity acquired a clear awareness of its capacity to know and transform nature and society; that is to say, to transform history by taking it into hand. This exercise of human reason appeared to be radically free in the measure that persons recognized themselves as able to change the conditions of their lives and to situate themselves differently within social relations.[27]

Thus the Enlightenment is viewed by Gutiérrez as a period of great promise in which growing self-consciousness stimulated people to perceive themselves as responsible for the shape of the world. History was seen as something people create rather than a product of divine, immutable laws. This crucial epistemological breakthrough led the way to a redefinition of political and economic life. There was a growing awareness that these vital spheres of life shaped the overall nature of society.

> The industrial revolution and the political revolution were in fact to appear more and more clearly, not as two processes which happened to

be contemporary or convergent, but as two movements depending one
on the other. As both advanced, their reciprocal involvement became
more evident. To transform history required a simultaneous transformation in nature and society. In this transforming praxis, there
is more than a new consciousness of the meaning of economic and
political action — there is a new way of being man [sic] in history.[28]

At face value these developments were positive accomplishments. The
"demystification" of nature and society was a precondition for economic
and political self-determination. To the extent that the Enlightenment
opened the way for new and more just social relationships it was a liberating
process.

According to Gutiérrez, however, the freedom promised by the Enlightenment was perverted and reduced to an unbridled, individualistic freedom
to function economically without restraint. The new dominant class, the
bourgeoisie, set out to reorder society in accord with its own socio-economic
interests. The so-called laissez faire capitalism associated with the bourgeois class really aimed to maximize their wealth and power as a social
class.

> The absolute principle that the economic activities of persons should
> be free led to the corresponding notion that freedom should also be
> absolute in the organization of the society to which they belong. In-
> dividual freedom is the first exigency.

The demands for individual freedom and social equality are thus
related to the new economic forms. Similarly, the right to private
property is fundamental for bourgeois society, for above all, this right
concerns the matter of ownership of the means of production. "The
freedom of industry," wrote G. de Ruggiero, "is the daughter of modern individualism; even more it is its favorite daughter." Social equality also has a clear economic reference: persons are equal in the moment of buying and selling. Furthermore, the formal equality is a
condition of mercantile activity.[29]

Such presuppositions gauge worth on the basis of personal initiative and
economic power. What remains unsaid, however, is that those who cannot
buy and sell are not socially equal in this system. They are lesser beings
with lesser freedoms. Yet the practitioners of capitalism turn a blind eye
to this fact. Never leaving the realm of abstraction, they fail to see the
destructive side of the system they so richly benefit from and fervently
promote.

Despite the claims of its advocates that capitalism is based on freedom
and egalitarianism, it depends on social inequality for its very existence.
As Cardoso and Faletto point out, social imbalance is a basic operative
principle of the system:

Capital itself is the economic expression of a social relation; it requires the existence of a set of persons working by wage — selling its labor force — and another group owning machines and money to buy raw material and to pay wages and salaries. On the other hand, such an "economic" relation supposes not only exploitation — and thus social mechanisms to assure domination — but some degree of stability and recurrence in the relations of exploitation.[30]

We are thus confronted with a seeming enigma: the egalitarian virtues of the Enlightenment that capitalism claims to have incorporated into its very fabric and logic produce inequality and injustice. Rather than uniting people with a common social purpose, it divides them along class lines.

As Gutiérrez and others have noted, capitalist values have dominated most Latin American countries since the time of their inception as independent nations. In many ways, the independence movements of the early nineteenth century were set in motion to achieve a more favorable economic climate for local elites and entrepreneurs who found colonial trade restrictions an impediment to their own desire for independent expansion. Liberation meant freedom to follow the dictates of capitalism unencumbered by financial ties to Spain's weakening mercantile economy. Despite the lyrics of nationalist myths, in many ways the wars of independence in the early nineteenth century had more to do with financial policies than they did with anti-monarchist sentiment or the liberation of Indians and blacks. As Gutiérrez indicates, the gap between real and fictitious history is wide:

> The liberal utopia promised the new countries a political organization based on freedom and modernity. A more or less ambiguous liberal ideology influenced the political constitutions. The break with Spanish domination and the entrance into a new situation of oppression in relation with the great capitalistic countries was the work of a white creole elite and of a few other sectors won over to the ideal of freedom. The poorer sectors, Indians, Blacks and *mestizos,* either had no participation or they had a passive participation, in many cases only sporadically. The freedom which the new political constitutions guaranteed did not reach the whole of society and was limited to favoring the privileges of the dominant groups at the service of the rising international bourgeoisie.[31]

These observations make it clear that the basic economic and political makeup of Latin America was not changed by independence. Instead of enriching colonial oppressors, the labor of ordinary people was channeled to serve the interests of national elites. Exploitation was simply given a nationalistic veneer.

Given the gap between political theory and socio-economic reality, it should come as no surprise that the level of nationalistic propaganda in most Latin American countries is high. Patriotism is declared the highest of virtues. Unfortunately the patriotism in question often equates with a blind faith in the beneficence of the status quo. Uncritically accepting the existing system, despite its deficiencies, becomes an index of loyalty while questioning what exists is tantamount to subversion. Such ideological messages have been constantly disseminated by the mass media, educational system, and, at least in the past, by the church.

Fortunately, however, the power of these ideological apparatuses is limited, since the experience of poverty tends to counterbalance their impact. This is precisely why Gutiérrez stresses the importance of "contradiction" among the poor as a crucial ingredient in their political consciousness that awakens them to the real nature of society despite the narcotic of propaganda. As Gutiérrez explains, the poor have always known in practical terms that the freedoms proclaimed in their countries' constitutions have little to do with their day-to-day lives:

> Everything was adorned and dissimulated by using a vocabulary of modern terms for political freedoms to fool some factions of the population, but little by little all the adornments were revealed to be lies. The movement for modern freedoms, democracy, and the universal and rational thought in Europe and the United States, meant for Latin America a new type of oppression and more cruel forms of despoilment of the poor classes.[32]

Gutiérrez feels that this experience of contradiction has had positive effects. There is a growing awareness among the oppressed that the so-called freedoms of capitalism only mean "more refined forms of exploitation of the very poorest — of the wretched of the earth."[33] He is convinced that this experience of contradiction has political implications that can reshape the socio-economic makeup of Latin America.

> Political consciousness is sharpened when the contradiction grows between an increasing aspiration to secure effective freedom and justice, and the existence of a social order which claims to recognize freedom and justice in law, but in reality denies them in countless ways to social classes, entire peoples and racial minorities.[34]

The growing recognition of many that capitalism cannot provide a meaningful life for the majority of Latin Americans has created what Gutiérrez calls a "critical suspicion" toward the present system. In his view, this explains why many of the oppressed are now engaged in a "revolutionary, militant search for the right conditions for the construction of a free, just society."[35]

Drawing from Paulo Freire's important works on popular education and consciousness raising, Gutiérrez considers the Latin American masses' experience of contradiction to be an indispensable step in the growth of their socio-political consciousness. He sees the process of focusing on the contradictions the oppressed experience in their lives as a pedagogical tool that exposes the deficiencies and deception of the dominant system. It helps them become conscious of their real position in society. They gradually perceive their uniqueness and become aware of how the values of the dominant sector are antithetical to their own well-being. Contradiction is the catalyst that forces the poor to analyze their context and begin "marching toward a society in which man will be free of every servitude and master of his own destiny."[36] This experience is the first step in the process of liberative praxis.

The Development and Dependency Theories

Gutiérrez claims in *A Theology of Liberation* that the social consciousness of the poor in Latin America is now "progressing from a partial and anecdotal understanding of its situation to a more complete and structural one."[37] This shift from vague discontent to informed criticism is due in many ways to the fact that political organizations, as well as basic Christian communities, often serve as study groups in which sophisticated socio-political theories are examined and discussed. As well as being more organized, the oppressed sector is also more attuned to the need for formal study of social structures if real change is to be achieved. As a theologian and member of a basic Christian community, Gutiérrez has read a great deal of socioeconomic theory. In the paragraphs that follow we shall briefly look at how some of the principal economic schools of thought in Latin America are approached in his writings.

In general terms, there are two schools of thought regarding the socioeconomic makeup of Latin America. One is the pro-capitalist thinkers who stand behind the so-called development theory. Certain Latin American social and economic theorists subscribe in varying degrees to what Gutiérrez calls "structural-functionalist categories"[38] of analysis that have been in vogue since the fifties and are now visible in such theories as supply-side economics. Generally trained in North American or European universities, they follow the theoretical models of development proposed by scholars such as Rostow, Parsons, Vekemans, and Berger. To varying degrees they believe socio-economic advancement will come about if Latin American countries imitate the more developed societies in the contemporary world. They see the economies and social structures of North America and Western Europe as paradigms that must be duplicated in Latin America in order to achieve progress.

During the fifties these believers in the free enterprise system took over national planning boards and ministries of finance. Supported by projects like the Alliance for Progress, which supplied technical advice and billions of dollars in aid, they set out to "rationalize" Latin America's economic structures and bring them more fully into the fold of modern international capitalism. They still exercise great power. Many are now senior ministers of government and actively promote a type of centrally controlled, highly disciplined capitalist system whose most notorious example is the national security state.

On the other side of the fence stand the proponents of the "dependency theory." Despite differences of opinion and distinct emphases, theorists like Cardoso and Faletto, Portes and Walton, Dos Santos, and Sunkel feel that the root cause of Latin America's poverty is the capitalistic system itself. To varying degrees, each advocates an alternative socio-economic system. Some employ Marxist analysis to arrive at this conclusion while others do not. Gutiérrez clearly feels that the dependency theory provides the most accurate analysis of Latin American economic structures. Its basic principles figure prominently in his early works. Yet, he retains a critical posture toward this school of thought, convinced that its theories must be deepened.

The Development Theory

Following the Second World War Latin American elites were convinced that a process of "inward development"[39] could industrialize their countries and help them arrive at a new era of prosperity. Many felt that their so-called backwardness was due to the continent's traditional reliance on natural resource exportation and agriculture for income. They also felt their countries were underdeveloped because of traditional social structures. A high percentage of people were outside the money economy. In Peru, Bolivia, and Ecuador large numbers of Aymara and Quechua *campesinos* relied on subsistence agriculture and barter in small, isolated villages. The apparent solution to these peoples' poverty was to induce them into a capitalist mode of production where the incentive of money and the cult of individual achievement would transform them into a more efficient, affluent social body. In effect, the proponents of capitalist development were saying that one of the primary causes of poverty was the traditional, collective way of life of the poor themselves. Once it changed poverty would be eliminated.

National planning agencies staffed by sociologists were established and given the mandate to "modernize" their countries. Agricultural production was increasingly controlled and capitalized by central governments. Peasant communities were forcefully restructured in order to integrate them into the national economy. Schools were established for the first time in indigenous communities; the schools were staffed by Spanish-speaking teachers who followed curricula prescribed by national ministries of education. Gutiérrez sums up the goals and ideas of the period as follows:

> To develop meant to be oriented towards a model abstracted from the more developed societies in the contemporary world. This model

was considered to be "modern society" or "industrial society." In achieving this goal, social, political, and cultural obstacles originating from the archaic political structures proper to underdeveloped countries — also referred to as "traditional societies" or "transitional societies" — had to be overcome. The underdeveloped countries thus were considered backwards, having reached a lower level than the developed countries. They were obligated, therefore, to repeat more or less faithfully the historical experience of the developed countries in their journey towards modern society.[40]

A process of urban expansion and cultural change was set in motion by government agencies. Lima, for example, changed from a quaint city of moneyed gentry to a metropolitan area with millions of people in less than fifteen years. The growing urban masses were told they were participating in a process of national development. Inadequate housing and wages were said to be momentary problems that would eventually be rectified as wealth trickled down to the working class. Hard work, patriotic fervor, and patience were the order of the day.

As Portes and Walton mention, none of the advocates of capitalist development was willing or able to recognize that "the brunt of sacrifices to be borne" was being placed squarely "on the shoulders of the masses."[41] In effect, the underpaid labor of an almost instant industrial proletariat was financing national "progress." The obvious fact that industrialization was creating an immense and impoverished working class seemed to escape the attention of elites. Social structures were indeed changing, but apparently few of the individuals responsible for the changes were cognizant of the real cost of this process. Former peasants who at least were able to survive in a system of subsistence agriculture were now at the mercy of a money economy. Transplanted to urban slums and bereft of the human support their cultures traditionally provided them, the poor were subjected to both monetary and spiritual impoverishment. As Gutiérrez has mentioned, these people found themselves in "a land of death...alien to their hopes."[42]

The development theory has influenced nearly every Latin American country's policies for economic development in the last thirty years. National industrialization has been the order of the day, and in countries like Peru, Chile, and Argentina it has often been promoted by military governments that have tolerated no discussion of its underlying principles or social finality. National development along capitalist lines is a quasi-religious concept one doubts only at the risk of being condemned as a blasphemer. As Portes and Walton point out, those who believed in this process never wavered in their conviction that it could deliver prosperity even though it was clearly generating misery. Poverty, at a magical future moment, would somehow disappear — presumably transmuted into well-being.

The doctrine of developmentalism has thus been adopted by authoritarian regimes in Latin America as the official ideology of inequality. This doctrine bypasses earlier ideological emphasis on the origins of inequality to affirm that, no matter what the causes of poverty are, it will not be overcome until certain measures are taken. A true solution to poverty and a gradual reduction of inequality must flow out of economic development. In order for this to occur, existing inequalities must be maintained and even expanded so as to facilitate concentration of income in the hands of the capitalist class and stimulate investment. After investment and production reach a certain level, their self-propelled dynamism will benefit the majority of the population by "filtering down" in the form of employment demand and higher wages.[43]

Initially, many of these policies seemed to promise eventual success. The alchemists who promised to change poverty into wealth and class-stratified societies into cohesive, middle-class nations seemed to have found an effective formula. A few countries experienced economic "booms," which augured well for the future. The Brazilian economy, for example, grew at a prodigious rate for several years. Although Peruvian development was less pronounced, the wages of workers grew substantially from 1968 until 1973. Unemployment was relatively low. A growing middle class seemed to prove that socio-economic progress was possible. The progress, however, was fleeting. As we have seen, the money in circulation had been loaned by international banks. When the orgy of borrowing was over in the late seventies, most Latin American countries had severe economic hangovers and no money in their pockets. Increased oil prices, the competition of the international market, and nearly uncontrollable inflation brought nascent industries to the point of collapse. As Gutiérrez points out, the theorists of modernization were working with a linear model of development. They were convinced that once the right structures and people were in place economic development would automatically "take off" on its own.

With the inevitable qualifications and variations, this theory yielded a model and an ideology of modernization which explained the transition of Latin American societies from traditionalism to modernism, from underdevelopment to development.[44]

In Gutiérrez's opinion, the developmentalist model never left "an abstract and ahistorical level" of analysis.[45] It was an erroneous and naïve theory whose disastrous results were inevitable. The fact that its advocates thought they could simply change their position in the world system and achieve economic parity with the First World was indicative of a lack of realism and solid analysis. Whether they were too enthusiastic or simply blinded by their loyalty to the principles of capitalism is a moot question.

First World nations were indeed eager to see greater industrialization in Latin America, but their concern was to exploit new sources of cheap labor. They were not about to accept so-called developing nations as real competitors on the international market.

As early as the 1960s many observers were beginning to realize that "the achievement of a more egalitarian or more just society" could not be "expected from capitalist development, especially in peripheral economies."[46] In the first place the cards were simply stacked against developing countries regardless of their most concerted efforts to enter the international market as full-fledged participants. Dependency on loans, foreign oil, and the vagaries of market prices almost invariably canceled out the few gains that were made. Secondly, development was actually increasing class stratification rather than minimizing it. What little capital developmentalist policies generated often went back to international banks, was exported by multinational firms, or was simply pocketed by national oligarchies. In short, there was not enough capital left to "trickle down" to the general population. The exploitative mode of capitalism was simply becoming more refined and ruthless, despite the fact that it was called "progress."

Social structures were indeed being changed and Latin American countries industrialized, but it became increasingly clear that the advancement of people was only a peripheral concern of national and international capitalists. Developmentalism was, in fact, a type of social deception, a new application of capitalist ideology that created a class of permanently impoverished industrial workers whose labor would create more wealth for the already wealthy. Development never eliminated the deeply ingrained classism and racism of Latin America. To the contrary, the effects of these social sins were exacerbated. Rather than suppressing the negative effects of capitalism, industrialization only produced a more virulent and deadly mutant.

The Dependency Theory

As Gutiérrez notes, the development theory "did not sufficiently take into account political factors, and worse, stayed on an abstract and ahistorical level." Thus he and others conclude that it was ultimately "unsound and incapable of interpreting the economic, social, and political evolution of the Latin American continent."[47] Based on the ideological values of the dominant sector and a linear, monetary understanding of progress, the development theory never really took stock of the history, culture, and political aspirations of the majority of people whose concept of development was distinct from that of elites. It became clear that abiding development could not be achieved by people in government ministries who were blinded by their faith in the capitalist system. Development had to flow from the poor themselves, from their self-perception and hopes as human beings and members of an oppressed class in search of liberation. To the extent that they were treated as manipulable masses and objects of ideological indoctrination, the social and even spiritual wherewithal for true development would be lacking.

A number of economists and sociologists began to speak of the disparity between what they call the "center" and "periphery" of the world market as both an economic and social problem. The unequal mode of exchange necessary for capital accumulation, which characterized the relationship between First and Third World nations, was being woven into the social fabric of developing countries. The disparity between "developed" and "developing" countries was reflected in a growing gap between national elites and masses in Third World countries themselves. The discrepancy between "center" and "periphery" was becoming a national as well as an international problem, as classism and the unequal distribution of wealth increased.

Analyzing trade patterns, the proponents of the dependency theory saw that Third World nations were being systematically exploited. The relationship between the "center" and "periphery" of international trade was skewed in favor of dominant countries. The modernization of poorer countries proposed by the advocates of the development theory was only making them more amenable to the needs of "center" countries for cheap labor and natural resources. The so-called backwardness of Third World countries was actually a reflection of their place in the capitalist system of production. Modernization and industrialization were causing dependence and economic disparity, not solving them. The International Monetary Fund and multinationals were dictating economic and political policy to supposedly sovereign governments. National elites generally acquiesced in the face of foreign domination as a price to be paid if they were to maintain their hegemony. Furthermore, they felt more allied culturally with the First World than they did with the poor of their own countries, whom they often perceived as deficient human beings inherently relegated to a subordinate role in society.

It became increasingly clear to many analysts that Latin America's poverty was not the result of inherent social "defects" and cultural "backwardness," as certain advocates of developmentalism had claimed. The continent's poverty was, and is, the result of dependence and the unjust social structures it produces. Gutiérrez makes it clear that understanding this dependence is the key to explaining Latin America's economic history and present social structures:

> This initial situation of dependence is the basis for a correct understanding of underdevelopment in Latin America. The Latin American countries are "from the beginning and constitutively dependent." For this reason their social structure is very different from that of the

center countries. It is necessary to determine carefully the differences between these two societies and to reformulate the concept which will allow us to analyze the situation and even the internal social structure of the peripheral countries.[48]

Gutiérrez knows from the history of his own country that Peru has been "constitutively dependent" since the time of the Conquest. Its resources have enriched foreigners, not the majority of Peruvians. The existence of poverty in a naturally rich country is not an enigma. It can be explained by analyzing the way capitalism works.

The elites who run the country put more trust in the beneficence of foreign capital than they do in the human wealth of the Peruvian people. They look outward for a socio-economic model, not inward to their fellow citizens. Clearly, dependency is more than an economic phenomenon. It is also a complex spiritual problem. As ardent believers in the ideology of capitalism, national elites willingly sell their nation's wealth in the name of "progress," thus perpetuating their own power and producing poverty. To do this requires that they be deaf to the cries of the oppressed as well as blind to the sinful effects of their own choices and actions as a social class. The dependency fostered by capitalism has twisted the perception and moral consciousness of the wealthy while inflicting untold suffering on the poor. By demonstrating the imperialistic nature of both international and local capitalism the exponents of the dependency theory went a long way in demystifying the propaganda of developmentalism. Its classist orientation and destructive results were exposed for what they really were. They showed that the rhetoric of developmentalism about equality and opportunity had nothing to do with the way the capitalist system actually worked. This information helped the poor realize that their situation of misery was not a product of their own debilities as the dominant sector would have them think. They were now able articulately to criticize the values and policies of those who controlled their lives. As Gutiérrez tells us, the dependency theory helped generate political resistance to the dominant class's ideology.

> Another expression of our Latin American people's new political awareness is their better grasp of the socio-economic realities of their continent. A great help here has been what is called the "theory of dependency" in economics and sociology, by which relationships of domination are basically reduced to class confrontation. Despite its shortcomings and gaps, this analysis has by and large been a boon. It is an attempt to rethink our distinctive historical process in categories peculiar to that process. It received its impetus from the liberation movements of the 1960s and contributed to the crystallization of those movements. It helped the popular class to reject the politics of compromise and conformism during that decade.[49]

During the 1960s popular political movements grew rapidly in Latin America as the poor began to organize. Stimulated by events in Cuba, the demand for economic justice and a radical restructuring of the prevailing economic system became a vocal, articulate cry that fired the popular imagination. At various times Brazil, Chile, Bolivia, and Peru seemed to be moving toward a type of socialism.

Unfortunately, those heady days were not to last long. As Gutiérrez tells us, "the birth of this movement, in its radical and moderate expressions alike, was most savagely repressed."[50] Multinationals, local elites, national armies, and those coopted by the dominant class joined forces to crush popular political movements. The power brokers took the offensive in defense of their "rights." Perhaps because they were somewhat idealistic and politically untested, many of those who advocated social change were forced to retreat. Nonetheless, they were neither routed nor eliminated. The growing class and economic consciousness of oppressed people did not disappear.

In Gutiérrez's opinion the insights of the dependency theory, along with growing political experience, helped many of the poor to arrive at something of a sociological "Copernican revolution." More importantly, they were now willing to fight against the injustice they and their fellows experienced. Their newly acquired knowledge had led to a qualitatively different type of political action among the poor with deeper and more challenging demands.

We had begun to perceive the "social disparity," as the specialists like to say, in our social structure — the life disparity, if they will permit us — and never again would the poor hesitate to defend their rights. Nor would blows and repression any longer deter them from their quest for a socialist way, their search for a genuine democracy.[51]

Gutiérrez is convinced that despite continued repression the "popular movement is better oriented, and better organized than it ever was before. It has new instruments of analysis at its disposal, and its intent is now clearly and specifically anticapitalist."[52]

Endowed with greater political maturity many in the popular movement no longer see dependency as a purely economic phenomenon. They are increasingly aware of its overall societal effect and class-related basis. These insights have helped the popular movement better appreciate the magnitude of the task before it and ground its strategies for social change in realistic class analysis. Furthermore, it is increasingly obvious to many people committed to social change, both Christian and non-Christian, that achieving real justice presumes a deep spiritual vision of life. It is precisely for this reason that Gutiérrez's most recent writings address the challenge of creating a spirituality of social transformation.[53] He is increasingly convinced that without a solid spirituality that incorporates both the experience of oppression and a firm belief in the power of faith, real social change will remain elusive.

Gutiérrez is fully aware that dependency is more than an external economic problem. It affects the life of Third World peoples on multiple levels. Well versed in the theories of Freud and Marcuse, he is convinced that dependency is also a cultural, political, and psychological phenomenon. These varied and complex facets of dependency must be taken into account in order to "avoid pseudo-interpretations and facile solutions"[54] of the phenomenon. More equitable economic exchange between nations or better prices for natural resources will ultimately not solve the problem, which lies within the dominant system itself. Gutiérrez maintains that the only effective way of overcoming dependency is to make a clean break with the system and values that cause it.

> Only a radical break from the status quo, that is, a profound transformation of the private property system, access to power of the exploited class, and a social revolution that would break this dependence would allow for the change to a new society, a socialist society — or at least allow that such a society might be possible.[55]

Before this can happen, however, the victims of dependency must come to terms with the dominant system. Oppressed peoples must take stock of the power of capitalist elites, the ideological processes they use to maintain their power, and how it affects or "penetrates" their own lives.

Subjected to intense ideological pressure, some of the poor have internalized the values of capitalism. Some blame their poverty on personal sloth or the cultural backwardness they supposedly suffer from, not the dominant system. Although many of the poor have achieved a marked degree of critical social consciousness and political will, more must be involved in the process of personal and social transformation. More of the poor must be convinced of their own worth. They need a stronger faith in themselves and the presence of God in their lives. They need to hear and share in the spirituality of their brothers and sisters committed to social change. Drawing from Freire's works, Gutiérrez believes that the oppressed must experience personal and political "conscientization" in order to grapple effectively with the ideological grip the ruling class exerts over their lives.

> In this process ... the oppressed person rejects the oppressive consciousness which dwells in him, becomes aware of his situation, and finds his own language. He becomes, by himself, less dependent and freer, as he commits himself to the transformation and building up of society.[56]

In the course of conscientization oppressed people begin to see the deceitfulness of the prevailing system and how it has warped their own lives.

Equipped with this knowledge the poor can fight an effective political battle against the dominant sector.

To Gutiérrez's mind the cry for justice in Latin America is the result of the growing self-knowledge of oppressed peoples. Because of the insights provided by the dependency theory, "popular education" projects, and the increased political activity they engender, many have come to see the relationship between their own exploitation and the dominant system more clearly. This explains why so many oppressed peoples are struggling for a radically new social order "truly free from servitude, and where they are the active shapers of their own destiny." The poor are looking for a "wholly new way for men and women to be human."[57] Thus, the poor want more than economic equality. They want to affirm their own values, history, and future. In Gutiérrez's terms, they are struggling for integral liberation.

NOTES

1. See Gustavo Gutiérrez, *The Power of the Poor in History: Selected Works*, trans. Robert R. Barr (Maryknoll, N.Y.: Orbis Books, 1983), p. 203.

2. This is also the fundamental thesis of Roger Haight's work *An Alternative Vision: An Interpretation of Liberation Theology* (Mahwah, N.J.: Paulist Press, 1985). This is one of the most incisive and scholarly works about liberation theology to be published to date by a North American.

3. Additional bibliographical material can be found in Robert McAfee Brown, *Makers of Contemporary Theology: Gustavo Gutiérrez* (Atlanta: John Knox Press, 1980), pp. 20–28. Albeit small, this work provides an excellent introduction to Gutiérrez's world and theology.

4. Luis Peirano, "Entrevista con Gustavo Gutiérrez," *Quehacer* (March 1980): pp. 115–116.

5. John Paul II, Opening Address (Puebla) III, 4[1209], as quoted in Gutiérrez, *The Power of the Poor*, p. 133.

6. Ibid., p. 85.

7. As quoted in *Resumen Semanal*, No. 327 (August 1, 1985): p. 1.

8. Alejandro Portes and John Walton, *Labor, Class and the International System* (New York: Academic Press, 1981), p. 183.

9. Ibid., p. 108.

10. Gutiérrez, *We Drink from Our Own Wells: The Spiritual Journey of a People*, trans. Matthew J. O'Connell (Maryknoll, N.Y.: Orbis Books; Melbourne, Australia: Dove Communications, 1983), p. 11.

11. Gutiérrez, *The Power of the Poor*, p. 84.

12. Ibid., p. 85.

13. Fernando Henrique Cardoso and Enzo Faletto, *Dependency and Development in Latin America*, trans. Marjory Mattingly Urquidi (Berkeley: University of California Press, 1979), p. 212.

14. Gutiérrez, *The Power of the Poor*, p. 217, note 47.

15. An excellent study of the origin and political "logic" of the national security state can be found in José Comblin's work *The Church and the National Security State* (Maryknoll, N.Y.: Orbis Books, 1979).

16. Cardoso and Faletto, p. 195.

17. Gutiérrez, *The Power of the Poor*, p. 92.

18. *Sendero Luminoso,* or, as it is often translated in English, *The Shining Path,* is a guerrilla movement that originated in the central mountain region of Peru in the early 1980s. Politically it follows a Maoist type of Marxism, albeit in a unique way. *Sendero Luminoso* has now spread to most parts of the country. Its tactics are both violent and irrational.

19. David Tejada, "América Latina: La deuda inmanejable," *Quehacer* 30 (August 1984): p. 54.

20. Portes and Walton, p. 134.

21. Cardoso and Faletto, p. 202.

22. Gutiérrez, *The Power of the Poor*, p. 117.

23. For a dated but still useful analysis of the policies of the military government of Velasco, see Abraham F. Lowenthal, ed., *The Peruvian Experiment: Continuity and Change under Military Rule* (Princeton: Princeton University Press, 1975).

24. Thomas Burns, *Peru National Reality, 1984,* p. 1. Mimeographed document written for the Maryknoll Fathers and Brothers, Peru Region.

25. Gustavo Gutiérrez, "Notes for a Theology of Liberation," *Theological Studies* 31 (1970): 352.

26. For an analysis of the semantic meaning of liberal capitalist values see Gustavo Gutiérrez and Richard Shaull, *Liberation and Change,* ed. Ronald H. Stone (Atlanta: John Knox Press, 1977), pp. 27–34.

27. Ibid., p. 27.

28. Gutiérrez, *Concilium* 96: pp. 62–63. Throughout the early translations of Gutiérrez's works the Spanish term *hombre,* which, at least in principle, is a gender inclusive term, is translated by the exclusive term "man." More recent translations of Gutiérrez use inclusive language.

29. Gutiérrez and Shaull, p. 31.

30. Cardoso and Faletto, p. 13.

31. Gutiérrez and Shaull, p. 70.

32. Ibid., p. 71.

33. Gutiérrez, *The Power of the Poor,* p. 186.

34. Gutiérrez, *Concilium* 93: p. 135.

35. Ibid.

36. Gutiérrez, *Theological Studies* 31: 250.

37. Gustavo Gutiérrez, *A Theology of Liberation: History, Politics and Salvation,* trans. and ed. Sister Caridad Inda and John Eagleson (Maryknoll, N.Y.: Orbis Books, 1973), p. 81.

38. Ibid., p. 82.

39. Ibid.

40. Ibid.

41. Portes and Walton, p. 129.

42. Gutiérrez, *We Drink from Our Own Wells*, p. 11.

43. Portes and Walton, pp. 128–129.

44. Gutiérrez, *A Theology of Liberation*, p. 83.

45. Ibid.

46. Cardoso and Faletto, p. xxiii.

47. Gutiérrez, *A Theology of Liberation*, p. 83.

48. Ibid., pp. 84–85.

49. Gutiérrez, *The Power of the Poor*, p. 78.

50. Ibid., pp. 78–79.

51. Ibid., p. 79.

52. Ibid., p. 78.

53. The two works in question are *We Drink from Our Own Wells: The Spiritual Journey of a People,* trans. Matthew J. O'Connell (Maryknoll, N.Y.: Orbis Books; Melbourne,

Australia: Dove Communications, 1983), and *On Job: God-Talk and the Suffering of the Innocent,* trans. Matthew J. O'Connell (Maryknoll, N.Y.: Orbis Books, 1987).

54. Gutiérrez, *A Theology of Liberation,* p. 87.
55. Ibid., pp. 26–27.
56. Ibid., p. 91.
57. Gutiérrez, *The Power of the Poor,* p. 29.

Chapter 2

The Cultural and Religious World of the Poor

> I want to inspire hope in you. To tell you you should love the land
> with its fruits — your seed, your animals, your tools. . . . I want to tell
> you you should love your culture, your songs, your language, your
> way of doing things, your family, your landscape. That along with
> the other poor you should make preparations and organize, because
> in unity alone is there strength. That sooner or later you or your
> children will possess the entire land because God has given it to all
> as a gift and a task. God is the sole true owner of the fields.
> — *Luis Vallejos, Archbishop of Cusco*[1]

These eminently theological words of Luis Vallejos are remarkably concrete
and, to venture a personal opinion, disarmingly beautiful. They are the
words of a man who championed the cause of *campesinos* by speaking
their language, sharing their food, and dancing in their fiestas. He saw
their history, daily work, and culture as expressions of an irrepressible will
to fuller life and liberation. As an archbishop he had great prestige and
power, but he went out of his way to be among and affirm Quechua-speaking
campesinos who have neither.

He championed land reform and bore the wrath of the wealthy who de-
nounced him as a Marxist agitator. He lived a life of evangelical simplicity
and died in an accident in 1982 on one of his frequent trips to a distant
Quechua community. At his funeral the poor openly wept at the loss of
a brother, and they themselves carried his body to its grave. Amid the
trappings of church ritual in a colonial cathedral they laid to rest a man
who had shared their dreams and been one among them. Dead but not
forgotten, his memory remains a potent force.

Vallejos and Gutiérrez were close friends and collaborated on many levels. When Gutiérrez's theology was criticized by conservative bishops and
Rome, Vallejos was an unswerving defender of its orthodoxy and pastoral

validity. The two men were convinced that theology had to flow from the lives of the poor themselves, whose culture and faith had to serve as its foundation. They realized that the exploited but still hopeful people around them spoke of a God present in history. This principle remains fundamental to Gutiérrez's theology. But the lives of these people and the God they witness to defy facile categorization. They are complex living processes that theological and analytical language can describe only in faltering terms. José María Arguedas, a Peruvian novelist and another close friend of Gutiérrez, points out that translating the culture and language of the poor in an intelligible way is a never-ending challenge.

To make real, to translate, to convert into a diaphanous and true current a language that seems distant; to communicate the foundation of our spirit in a foreign language — that is the hard and arduous task before us.[2]

It is a task, however, to which both Arguedas and Gutiérrez have directed nearly all of their energy. Both have gone to remarkable lengths to distill the truths expressed in the culture, symbols, and religiosity of the poor. Their commitment to this labor is not that of the impartial observer or cultural anthropologist, but that of individuals who see their fate inextricably bound up with the struggle of the poor for full humanity.

Popular Culture and Religion in Gutiérrez's Theology

In *A Theology of Liberation* there is a classic bibliography on popular culture and religiosity.[3] Since the book's publication in the early 1970s the number of studies of these phenomena has grown at a prodigious rate. Nonetheless, Gutiérrez has kept abreast of the latest scholarship. This has helped him avoid two unfortunate tendencies evident in certain analyses: romanticism, which ultimately trivializes the complex nature of the phenomena, and the extremes of the secularization theory, which postulates the inevitable Westernization of cultures and demise of religion.

As Gutiérrez points out in *The Power of the Poor in History,* in the mid-1970s he and his colleagues in the Las Casas Center, particularly Tokihiro Kudó and Raúl Vidales, set out to study popular religion in detail so as to better understand its implications for liberative praxis. This innovative project stemmed from a "refusal to accept simplistically the validity of the secularization process in Latin America, in spite of the spirit then in vogue."[4] Gutiérrez could no doubt see that the so-called secularization of Latin America had more to do with the wishful thinking of certain social scientists than it did with reality. What they discovered was a multilayered world of belief that changed their own assumptions about the role of religion in the life of ordinary Peruvians.

Gutiérrez is aware of the all-pervasiveness of religion in his own society. Catholicism is simply part of the atmosphere that most people take for granted. Nearly 95 percent of Peruvians classify themselves as Roman Catholics, although only 15 percent are religiously active. As early as the 1920s José Carlos Mariátegui, a journalist and Marxist theorist, observed that the religious beliefs of ordinary people have a profound sociological impact that anyone interested in social change must take into account. Gutiérrez paraphrases Mariátegui's ideas in *The Power of the Poor in History:*

> We have to take into consideration what Mariátegui called the "religious factor" in the life and history of the people of Peru. What we call popular piety is one of its expressions, but it is not the only one. The "religious factor," unfortunately, has frequently been, and still is today, a stumbling block to the people's advance in the perception of its situation of oppression. Much popular piety still reflects the dominant ideology, and any "religious populism" that ignores this is to be avoided. We are faced with a complex reality here, and our approach must take the complexity into account.[5]

Like Mariátegui, whose ideas we shall examine in the next chapter, Gutiérrez clearly views culture and religion critically. He believes there are negative and positive characteristics of these phenomena that require differentiation.

Gutiérrez never loses sight of the deeper and more positive facets of religion. He refuses to summarily dismiss it as a tool of ideological oppression. Critically understood and appropriated, religion can help the poor better understand society, their place in it, and the uniqueness of their experience. Under the right circumstances, it can even call forth resistance to the established order. Gutiérrez's view of popular religion generally coincides with that of Mariátegui, whose ideas Jeffrey Klaiber, a scholar of Peruvian religious history, summarizes as follows:

> Mariátegui perceived religion as a dynamic and intuitive element in people which inspires them to act and sustains their actions. In periods of social transition religion can even act in opposition to the dominant culture by offering people a vision of a new order as an alternative to the present one. In order to give religion a broader meaning than ordinary, Mariátegui preferred to subsume religion within the concept of "myth."[6]

It is the "mythical" element of religion that interests Gutiérrez, that is, its dynamic, forward-looking characteristic according to the meaning Mariátegui assigns to the term. Woven into an overall strategy of social change, religion can provide the indispensable spiritual motivation for liberative praxis.

Gutiérrez and the people who work with him in the Las Casas Center have tried to understand religion contextually, that is, as part of a larger social matrix. The Las Casas Center is staffed by people committed to social change who study sociology, economics, and popular religion in the midst of the poor rather than from a "neutral" distance. Their analyses, like the one done by Vidales and Kudó that we shall shortly examine, have a pastoral purpose. They are meant to help the poor, particularly those who are members of the Christian community, to better understand their own lives and values.

They approach culture and religion respectfully, cognizant that these social phenomena speak of powerful forces within the human psyche. They avoid the crass empiricism that has often flawed studies of culture and religion done by both "structural-functionalist"[7] and Marxist social analysts who are hobbled by the same empiricist biases, namely that religion and culture can somehow be isolated and completely categorized. Certain Marxists, of course, suffer from the added prejudice of considering religion a "regressive" phenomenon. A useful summary of the problems inherent in the empiricist tradition of social research can be found in an unexpected source — Edward Schillebeeckx's monumental work on christology:

> Because of the predominance of scientific thought in Western culture, this symbolic thinking in religious faith is often connected with the infancy of mankind, as the result of a one-sided predilection for what is often positivistic "instrumental reason." Religious language is allowed to have emotional, but not cognitive value. In that case "cognitive" is identified ... with an understanding which is essentially directed towards regularities, causal explanations and deductions. And symbolic knowledge has no cognitive or truth value except as "childish thought." This evaluation follows simply and solely from the fact that symbolic thinking is not subject to any empirical control; for that reason it is said to be "mythical group-thinking of primitives."[8]

As Gutiérrez and his colleagues know from experience, the religious and symbolic activities of the poor are hardly indicative of "childish thought." They are expressions of highly sophisticated and, in every sense of the word, cognitive processes. Yet one can grasp this fact only by living among the poor. Analyses of culture and religion done from a discreet and "impartial" distance all too frequently lead to superficial and erroneous conclusions.

Although the religiosity of the poor is a visible force in their lives, few analysts, be they social scientists or pastoral theologians, have adequately understood its role and nature in Latin America. As Kudó points out, this failure is often the result of methodological prejudices similar to those Schillebeeckx enumerates. Many analysts objectify religiosity, thus losing sight of its inter-active, inter-subjective qualities. Religiosity, like culture, is not an object; it is a human quality that can be understood only in terms of its bearers. As Kudó makes clear, religiosity is a multidimensional social phenomenon. To grasp its real meaning we must examine its agents along with their socio-economic context and history.

The effort in Latin America to understand the religiosity of the poor with its complexity and depth is beset by diverse obstacles. In certain scientific circles it is examined only in terms of a particular discipline, or from an imported theoretical framework that is not sufficiently attentive to the Latin American context. The multidimensional quality of the religious factor in a continent of oppression and resistance goes unrecognized. Furthermore, at times the possibility of evaluating religiosity from a theological and pastoral angle is dismissed. Thus, a methodological reductionism develops. For example, some insist on locating religion principally in the cultural realm, thus segregating it from economic and political factors without taking into account how the religiosity of the poor develops in the midst of a conflictive social reality.[9]

Kudó views religiosity as a part of oppressed peoples' lives which flows out of their self-perception and socio-political environment. The only way to adequately understand their religiosity is to live among them and see its "multidimensional quality." This requires more than mere presence. It is a question of a real commitment to oppressed peoples and an affective proximity to their cause. Precisely for this reason the members of the Las Casas team live and work among the poor, not temporarily nor for the sake of observation, but because they wish to struggle with them in the process of liberation.

On the basis of both experience and social scientific data, Gutiérrez and his co-workers are aware that religion, especially in a class-stratified society like Peru, can be a highly plastic, almost "dualistic" phenomenon. When religious rituals and symbols are monopolized by the ruling class as they traditionally have been in the Catholic Church of Latin America, religion often abets oppression. Yet, to the extent that the poor maintain some sort of autonomous symbolic life, the religion that gives it form and expression can be a powerful counterforce to the dominant ideology. As Gutiérrez points out in *The Power of the Poor in History,* we are dealing with an ambivalent reality:

> *The Latin American people is a Christian people, but it is also an exploited people.* Within this duality we find the ambivalence of popular religiosity, but also its liberating potential. We cannot forget that the dominant classes who oppress this people use Christianity to justify their privileges, but neither can we forget that the suffering of an oppressed people is revealed in popular expressions of faith. In them we find a resistance and a protest against domination, as well as a vigorous witness of hope in the God of the Bible.[10]

The crucial question then is to distinguish between the negative and positive characteristics of religious practice. But this can be done only by studying the broader socio-economic context in which the poor live out their religious lives. Whether religion is oppressive or liberative in a class-stratified society depends on the people who shape its content and expression, since the beliefs and rituals of the rich and poor are distinct and have a different social purpose.

Kudó recommends that the culture and religiosity of the poor be considered in terms of "the process of transformation of the historical conditions of domination and alienation of the people." This requires determining where "these phenomena are going and how to move forward"[11] with them in terms of social change. He suggests that the varied aspects of the culture of the oppressed be analyzed "historically." Because we are dealing with phenomena that are "spontaneous, cumulative, inorganic, but, at the same time, creative and dynamic aspects of the reality the masses experience in their daily lives,"[12] we need a touchstone, a criterion to gauge their positive and negative effects. For Kudó this criterion is the ability or inability of these phenomena to move the poor forward in their historical struggle for liberation.

> Popular culture is a product of history, an accumulated mix of elements whose origin lies both within the people themselves and the forces that affect them; it is a fragile mix, contradictory and unstable from the point of view of rational coherence, articulation, and organicity. It must always be approached with a hierarchy of values.[13]

In a manner of speaking, the culture and religiosity of the poor "do" things. They shape people's perception of the world for better or worse. They can either help the oppressed understand themselves in a more conscious way or help obfuscate their real situation. Kudó proposes, then, that culture and religiosity be understood and judged in terms of their ability to raise the historical and political consciousness of the poor.

Gutiérrez and Kudó realize that culture and religion in Latin America must be discussed as components of a social system built on class stratification and a capitalist mode of socio-economic production. Their perspective flows from an inevitable recognition that the division of labor characteristic of capitalism exerts a powerful psycho-social influence on each member of society. As Kudó puts it:

> We should not forget that the symbolic or cultural universe does not escape the effects of social conflict or the class struggle. As a result, to speak of culture globally can mystify the concrete social relations of production. For this reason, each time we speak of the "dominant" culture and "dominated" subcultures, culture must be specified by a theory of social classes if we want to say anything real, historical,

and concrete about the individuals who live and act it out. Used ahistorically and without a class perspective, the term "culture" does not help the investigator.[14]

In a society like that of Peru we are confronted with different cultures and religious beliefs that correspond to class-specific socio-economic roles. The culture of the dominant sector is clearly not that of the oppressed, despite its massive diffusion and ideological role as a social norm. The same applies in the religious realm. The beliefs of oppressors and oppressed are distinct, although there is a degree of contact and mutual influence. The meaning of the terms in question, then, is determined by the history and social position of their active subjects.

Kudó points out that the rich view the world in terms of their hegemony and its preservation while the poor see it in terms of powerlessness and sheer survival. We are confronted with what he calls two distinct processes of signification that inevitably influence a person's cultural and religious identity.

If the social aspect of life means, in our view, daily reality seen from the angle of relations of power between distinct human groups, the rich and the poor, then the "cultural" aspect of life relates to the same reality, but seen from the angle of relationships of signification. Since, then, concrete people, the rich and poor, live in social conditions in this society which are not only unequal but distinct, in the final analysis concrete people, viz., the rich and poor, have a distinct sense of life and different ways of relating with nature, other groups of people, and themselves.[15]

Clearly, any approach to culture and religion that fails to take the cognitive effects of class stratification into account misses the mark. Such a perspective can only lead to abstract and idealist definitions unrelated to the people and forces that shape culture and belief.

In Peru it is obvious that the projection of the dominant sector's bourgeois culture and particular version of Catholicism as socio-cultural norms is part of an ideological process that denies or covers over a whole realm of experience, namely that of the poor. The "normative" culture of the dominant sector serves as a gauge that measures people's participation in the "real" world. Those who ascribe to the reigning system are "integrated" and "modern" while those who are not are "marginalized" and "backward." The inference is that those with higher levels of consumption and employment are simply more advanced and sophisticated. Their position in the upper echelons of society is due to the superiority of their culture.

One frequently hears references to the culture and the activity of the dominant urban sector as norms or standardized models used to determine the lack of consumption, employment, and integration into the institutions of the dominant culture. As is obvious, this model is totally ahistorical and, from a cultural point of view, leads to an absurd type of self-alienation . . . in the name of modernity and progress.[16]

Such a posture avoids taking a hard look at the way class-stratified societies really work. It is primarily the socio-economic and class position of people that determines their degree of "integration" into the dominant system. The "standard" and ahistorical cultural model Vidales and Kudó refer to is really the self-serving self-image of the dominant sector that justifies the exploitation of "non-persons," that is, those who are "not considered human by the present social order."[17] Being culturally and religiously "backward," their labor and lives can be utilized by the dominant sector for its own ends.

The real interest in culture and religion on the part of the members of the Las Casas Center is ultimately strategic. Vidales and Kudó suggest that when we examine the socio-economic life of a class-stratified society we observe certain "fissures"[18] in its facade of cultural and religious uniformity established by the ruling class. These "fissures," which are evident in the language, values, and symbols of the poor, develop because they retain an alternative culture and religiosity distinct from those of the hegemonic sector.

In terms of our epistemological perspective, we have said that we cannot study popular religiosity except in terms of its socio-economic and political implications. For this very reason we cannot consider religion a neutral or ineffectual element and, at the same time, appreciate its constructive role. This very stance requires a serious effort to appreciate what we have called "the depth of the people's soul." To be able to arrive at a point where we can point out its structures, its function, the deep world of its myths, its symbols, its linguistic qualities, etc., means beginning the task [of analysis] where the system has not been totally able to take control of popular [cultural] production, at the deeper levels of popular culture.[19]

The challenge, then, is to move beyond social phenomena to the people who embody them. The cultural and religious life of the poor points the way to an alternative vision of life, a deep and contrary current capable of eroding the structures of domination. Understanding and tapping its force is a difficult task, but without the power it offers, real social change with "body and soul" is impossible.

The members of the Las Casas Center are aware that there is no "pure" form of popular culture or religiosity. The beliefs of the oppressed are shaped to some degree by the ideology of the dominant sector or, in Gramscian terms, "partially penetrated" by the ideological messages that are constantly disseminated in society. This is an inevitable result of inter-class socio-economic tension.

Not all the aspects of popular culture are necessarily liberating, far from it. The people constantly suffer from the pressure of the dominant ideology. The popular appropriation of these ideological messages that are pounded into them is generally synonymous with an increase of palliatives for their present misery, as an illusory refuge or opium.[20]

Nonetheless, they feel that popular culture and religion, albeit "partially penetrated," offer a "unique vantage point for understanding and shoring up"[21] the resistance of the poor to the dominant sector and its ideology.

Fundamentally, the interest of the members of the Las Casas Center in culture and religiosity stems from a desire to understand better the poor who, as active historical subjects, carry in themselves the motivation for radical social change. As Kudó notes, religion in particular is a crucial part of the poor's "lived experience" that must be included in any effective revolutionary strategy.

The reassessment or, better said, the revitalization of popular religiosity in Latin America can be construed ... as an integral part of the process of rediscovering the people [pueblo] as subjects of their own history. In this perspective, the interest in popular religiosity, without mentioning its value as part of daily life, is an important aspect of the epistemological question that necessarily arises within a theory of revolution rooted in the historical practices of an oppressed and resistant people. It is a question of what is called the "mass line" [*línea de masas*]: i.e., how to recover, respond to, synthesize, and give back what the people experience here and now.[22]

Vidales and Kudó go on to state that the "reevaluation" of popular culture and religion they have participated in ultimately stems from a desire to ground revolutionary praxis in the values and experience of ordinary people:

The most important thing is that the very processes of [popular religiosity], within an authentic perspective of liberation, have set reflection and suspicions in motion ... about the interrelation, evolution, role, etc. ... of religious practice within a movement of emancipation, complex as it is, ... for the process of liberation of our people.[23]

Although the studies of culture and religion initiated by the members of the Las Casas Center are still "in process," it is clear that they have gone to great lengths to understand their deeper qualities and incorporate their findings into a strategy for liberative praxis.

When Gutiérrez speaks of "rereading" and "rewriting" history, he implies recasting it in terms of the cultural values and beliefs of the oppressed despite their complexity. The project of "reevaluation" initiated by the members of the Las Casas Center is a first step in this endeavor meant to allow the poor to voice their own self-understanding and hopes for the future. As we shall see in the next section, the inhabitants of Lima's slums can be quite articulate. Their opinions are sometimes disconcertingly sharp and incisive given the burdens of poverty and ideological oppression they endure.

Data and Observations

Gutiérrez and his colleagues in the Las Casas Center insist that the call to liberative praxis will only make sense to the poor if it is expressed in their language. To that end, two members of the staff trained in sociology and theology, Tokihiro Kudó and Raúl Vidales, set out to listen to them. They developed a survey in the mid-1970s that was administered to several hundred residents of Lima's *pueblos jovenes* representing a cross-cut of various age groups and occupations. The questionnaire used simple responses and open self-expression to provide a broad yet "scientific" picture of oppressed people's culture and beliefs.

As one would expect in a *pueblo joven,* the majority of the adults interviewed, nearly 75 percent, were not born in Lima, but rather emigrated from the Peruvian *sierra* and *altiplano.* Attracted by the propaganda of developmentalism, they flocked to the city in the fifties and sixties in search of jobs. In effect, the majority of adult residents in the *pueblos jovenes* are transplanted *campesinos.* In a multi-cultural country like Peru, this factor has special implications. Many inhabitants of *pueblos jovenes* come from Quechua/Aymara-speaking areas. As Kudó points out, beyond the question of the linguistic identity of these people, there is also "an entire cultural world which exhibits the characteristics of the indigenous peasant of the Peruvian Andean region."[24] Although they know enough Spanish to function in Lima and quickly learn how to survive in an urban context, their cultural and religious values are shaped by an agrarian and communal experience of life distinct from that of the bourgeoisie and long-standing urban workers.

Because of their origins in indigenous and rural areas of the country, the majority of people in *pueblos jovenes* have been exposed to "social relations of production of a semi-feudal or semi-colonial sort."[25] In terms of early socialization, then, they have experienced cultural and linguistic discrimination as well as class stratification and conflict from childhood on. Most people had received little or no formal education. According to Kudó's calculations, only a bare majority of industrial workers could effectively read or write, while 68 percent of the peddlers and part-time laborers and 64 percent of the housewives were illiterate.

The members of the Las Casas team quickly found that the inhabitants of the *pueblos jovenes* display a socio-religious consciousness with complex characteristics. Kudó points out that many of the poor have obviously assimilated certain values of the dominant sector. At the same time, however, they have also managed to resist the ideological pressures of the ruling class in subtle ways. The culture and religion of the poor seem to be inextricably bound up with this mix of oppression and opposition. Rather than being static and immutable, they constantly change and assume different characteristics.

> Popular consciousness, that is, the social consciousness of the dominated popular classes, is, by definition, partially dominated, alienated, penetrated, and partially specific, autonomous, and resistant in terms of the ideology of the dominant class. In other words, cultural penetration and cultural resistance are two faces of the same historical reality of oppressed peoples. If domination-oppression and resistance-liberation are dialectical terms in permanent tension within a concrete historical process, *it is impossible, in an isolated way, to measure the force of domination on one hand and that of resistance on the other.*[26]

On the basis of his data, Kudó feels that the consciousness of the oppressed sector, with its various cultural and religious facets, must be understood as part of a larger historical process, that is, as part of the dialectical struggle between oppressor and oppressed that is constantly waged in Peruvian society. In the survey some people spoke of their political situation and faith in terms reminiscent of a hierarchical religious structure. They spoke of their poverty as fated by God. At the same time others held strong views about the necessity for radical social change and voiced their hope using religious concepts.

The study clearly demonstrates that culture and religion are potent forces that play a crucial role in the struggle between social classes in Lima. Because they shape the values that define society's purpose, the dominant sector invests considerable energy in order to control culture and religion "in defense of their privileges."[27] The ideological apparatuses of the dominant sector are constantly used "to oppress the consciousness of the poor with justifications of the present situation (cultural penetration)." Organized religion continues to be a "constitutive element of [ideological] explanation and justification"[28] in this process when it helps disseminate ahistorical and apolitical beliefs.

As Vidales and Kudó point out, when it is controlled by the dominant sector, religion produces "a sacralization of the established order."[29] It is used to proclaim the superiority of the status quo, which is supposedly consonant with divine will. Religion becomes a "civic activity" utilized to demonstrate the morality and legitimacy of the prevailing order. The two analysts explain the deeper causes of this phenomenon as follows:

> In effect, the [dominant sector] needs to legitimate itself in its own eyes and in the eyes of everyone; it has to demonstrate that it is at the service of democracy, of humanization, of liberty, etc.... In this way the "religious inversion" of the system comes about, its sacralization. At this level the use the system makes of certain rites and religious practices is not especially important, particularly on an official level. What is more important is the recuperation, utilization, and exploitation of symbols, beliefs, myths, and popular rituals.[30]

Because symbols and beliefs play such a crucial role in generating self-identity and loyalty to a social system, the dominant sector constantly dramatizes and affirms its hegemony with rituals. In Peru the general population is constantly exposed to well orchestrated religious and civic ceremonies meant to legitimate and strengthen those who benefit from the status quo. In Vidales and Kudó's opinion, the dominant sector's interest in culture and religion is part of an effort to appropriate their "cultural surplus value." Controlled by a ruling class, they offer efficient "internalizing channels of domination"[31] which "serve the dominant class as instruments to exercise and prolong their domination."[32]

The members of the Las Casas Center found that religion is most often utilized to dress the status quo in an aura of morality and orderliness. The poor are told through different ideological apparatuses that they must live in a patient, disciplined, and fraternal way and reproduce society as it presently exists. Unfortunately, these commendable virtues are twisted in such a way that they ultimately justify oppression and legitimate class stratification. They dull the social consciousness of the poor to the oppressive nature of the society they live in and provide pretexts for exploitation by the dominant sector.

> Through our process [of analysis] and the group work we mentioned, we are able to state that a specific way of presenting the Christian religion and its message to exploited classes has played an important role in generating a type of religious conduct among them that is ahistorical and apolitical.
>
> Fundamental elements such as "unity," "peace," "order," "liberty," "love for one's enemies," "the will of God," etc. have, in point of fact, acted, among other things, as *intrusive channels and mechanisms* of ideological legitimation that justify the established social order to the extent that they have deprived these messages of their dialectical force of protest and historical transformation.[33]

The ideological use of religion thus dissipates the transformative power of virtues that are "captured and manipulated in favor of the dominant system."[34] Socially decontextualized, they have no dialectical force. They help reproduce the prevailing unjust order rather than changing it.

Vidales and Kudó found, naturally enough, that the more the poor accept the established order as rational and moral, the less inclined they are to question it. Many residents in the *pueblos jovenes* often display a "functional" attitude toward the way their society works. They simply accept it for what it is and view their misery and exploitation as inevitable facts of life.

More concretely, we can say that when they were questioned about the task of immediately and concretely confronting the present situation of misery and oppression, seemingly, in an overwhelming way, a functional mentality develops among the poor in terms of the present capitalist system regardless of sex or age. In effect, the ideology of the dominant sector of society is present with all its force among the popular urban sectors; on one level the oppressed become "realistic" in the sense of "losing a larger hope" or of "no longer dreaming," because they begin to reason according to the logic of domination.[35]

Not surprisingly, the study found the most pronounced acceptance of the status quo among students and independent workers such as artisans.

The degree of cultural penetration by the present dominant class appears greatest in the consciousness of those poor who are obliged to work individually in the world of competition (in the capitalist market system), not to mention students who, being involved in a directly ideological area, are powerfully subjected to the influence of the dominant ideology of scientific neutrality, the efficacy of encyclopedic knowledge, progress, and social development without conflict, etc.[36]

These groups were more inclined to believe that by emulating the "virtues" of the ruling class, they could break out of their current oppression. Hard work, individualism, and knowledge were seen as antidotes to their present situation of poverty. In the case of the students, it is quite clear that they learned these notions from their teachers. Both students and independent workers were often incapable of seeing "the flagrant contradictions of the present system"[37] and prone to blame their misery and that of their fellow poor on self-inflicted failure and backwardness.

A large number of people interviewed often engaged in religious activities as a way of manipulating spiritual powers whose good will they deemed necessary for continued health and social well-being. The residents of Lima's slums use a wide array of religious practices to shelter themselves from the harshness and injustice they experience in daily life.

In general terms, the religiosity of the masses does not aim to "transform" life. Rather it serves to help them obtain empirical results or to provide solutions to the problems presented by daily life (the essence and finality of magic).

> Our hypothetical conclusion is that the meaning and principal function of popular religiosity are those of a great defense mechanism, perhaps the most important one in rural and marginalized areas, against the anxiety and insecurity [experienced by] ordinary persons. This fact explains the essence of the popular religion that the majority of our people practice today: externally it is Catholicism and internally it is magic.[38]

Yet Vidales and Kudó are careful to point out that even the "magical" qualities of popular Catholicism require detailed examination and should not be summarily dismissed as atavisms. Despite the judgment of some observers, they are not the result of "cultural backwardness, but rather are due to the structural conditions of society that allow them."[39] Furthermore, many forms of popular religion were created and fostered by the institutional church, which has employed them for its own ends. So-called "folk religion" is far more complex than one might imagine. Whether a person agrees with it or not, it is a vital sphere of activity for the poor, providing them with a way of understanding and coping with an oppressive existence. It must be approached respectfully with a minimum of prejudice. Perhaps the only people who truly have a right to judge its deficiencies and merits are the poor themselves.

Not surprisingly, the members of the Las Casas Center found that popular religion is more prone to act as an alienating force in societies where the political consciousness and will of the majority have been effectively repressed by the dominant sector.

> Within the global framework of a dependent capitalist formation, like that of Latin America and Peru, among the traditionally exploited popular sectors, with little or no historical and political consciousness, with weak or no active participation in the transformation of the dominant socio-economic and political system, popular religion plays an alienating role. And, to the extent that it helps maintain a mythical, ahistorical, and apolitical consciousness sacralizes the established order and ultimately legitimates it.[40]

In such a situation popular religion can produce a sense of resignation to prevailing inequalities. In Marxian terms, it can function as an "opium" that diminishes the pain of oppression. Yet our authors are aware of another facet of religion that Marx himself alluded too. As well as being a stupefying drug, it can also be a subtle form of protest.

Despite the efforts of the dominant sector to control the poor, they still retain a degree of independence since their experiences of life do not coincide with the images of normality engendered by the dominant ideology. The inevitable "fissures" in ideological processes Vidales and Kudó mention have crucial implications for the social role of religion and explain its unexpected ability to mobilize resistance to the status quo. Whether religious practices display oppressive or liberative qualities depends on the consciousness of oppressed peoples, the state of inter-class relations, and the desire of the poor for social change. All these factors interactively shape the character of religious expression.

Their basic conclusion is that cultural and religious phenomena must be analyzed in terms of a given historical situation. In Kudó's words, "There does not exist, in general, anything that is immutably and ahistorically good or bad for oppressed people."[41] It is not the definition or abstract nature of cultural and religious activities that interests them, but how these processes are lived out in a historical, changing situation of class struggle. Kudó spells out their position as follows:

> The religious practice of an oppressed people, in dialectical relationship with its global social activity, will translate itself into a range of behavioral patterns, attitudes, and opinions that will oscillate between active resistance and total submission, between self-liberation and captivity, passing through a series of loose complaints to unorganized protest. That is to say, one should not believe that all the elements of oppressed people's religiosity relate to positive protest, nor that all of them are absolutely alienated and alienating; to the contrary, the same religious or cultural element can develop a liberating potential or become an anti-popular element within a determinant set of circumstances as regards popular struggle.[42]

Thus, the criterion the members of the Las Casas Center use in gauging cultural and religious phenomena is their impact on liberative praxis. They refuse to condemn even the seemingly "magical" elements of popular religiosity or uncritically affirm them. In their opinion, the most superstitious facets of cultural Catholicism are "not necessarily and absolutely negative for the suffering masses."[43] It is always a question of how these religious practices affect people in a specific setting. This same flexible and contextual approach to cultural and religious phenomena is visible in Gutiérrez's own theological writings.

In discussions with the inhabitants of various *pueblos jovenes* and in their analysis of statistical data, the members of the Las Casas Center observed that the poor do not assimilate the socio-religious values of the dominant sector in an undifferentiated and direct way. Rather they appropriate them in terms of their own circumstances of poverty and oppression. Despite the dominant sector's ideological use of religion to generate belief in a common, inter-class social order with equality for all, there is an element of critical self-awareness evident in certain religious practices of the poor that display what might be called a "we-them" consciousness with important socio-political implications.

> In other words, the religious factor does not necessarily impede the perception by the poor of the social relations they really live out. There is a clear awareness of the distance between "them" and "us" in the very terrain of religion. These social relations of production are lived out in their totality in the lives of the poor both rationally and religiously, socially as well as culturally, precisely because these suffering people are both exploited and believing, in an indistinguishable way.[44]

Thus, despite a certain degree of ideological penetration, the religious practices of the poor can, under the right circumstances, serve as an "implicit political protest of oppressed peoples."[45]

The vast majority of people interviewed stated that there was a profound difference between the religious beliefs and values of distinct classes or, in the words of one person, between " 'us' and 'them,' " between those who are faithful to the saints and those who do not need God, between the poor and the rich."[46] In Kudó's opinion, such sentiments, couched as they are in religious language, display a high level of class consciousness and an unambiguous critique of the dominant sector. In fact, religion in the *pueblos jovenes* of Lima seems to be a crucial factor in helping the poor "perceive the instinctive social and cultural differences between the two groups that arise from a situation of historical conflict."[47] In Peru, where political language and activity are tightly controlled by an elite, religious terms and practices often serve as substitutes for political protest. When the poor claim that the rich "do not need God," they are making a political as well as a religious statement.

The analysts of the Las Casas Center found that many of the poor are often able to "short circuit" the ideological messages they were exposed to in a way that contradicts their primary purpose. Concepts like "fraternal love" and "equality before God" used by the dominant sector's religious apparatus for ideological ends had, under certain circumstances, the effect of helping the poor better understand their own position in society and appreciate the differences that separate their values and world from those of the dominant sector.

> It is also possible to say that for the majority of people...the content of [concepts like] "equality before God" is an obviously positive element for the revindication of their right to life. The bourgeois idea of the abstract equality of isolated individuals without distinction between rich and poor is appropriated in this context by the poor and believing sector in an original way: the God of the poor demands real fraternity from those "few" who "forget" the rights of the poor,

those who "disdain" the poor or "mistreat" them, etc., thus denying, in fact, the dignity of the poor as "children of God created in his image," etc.[48]

We are dealing here with a complex process in which the ideological religious messages of the dominant sector are reinterpreted and redirected against the very people who hope to capitalize on them. The poor reappropriate them in terms of their own context and class consciousness.

The Las Casas team found that over 88 percent of the inhabitants of the two urban zones agreed that "God cannot be in agreement with the present situation of inequality between people" in Peruvian society. The vast majority thought that the fundamental problem with the rich is that "they do not think about God...who does not want oppressed, trampled, suffering, and hungry people in this world." Ninety-eight percent stated that labor conflicts were "perfectly compatible with Christian love" and felt that unions could be an expression of the "right of the poor to bring about love for one's neighbors." Ninety-one percent were in total agreement that the poor could seize unoccupied but privately owned land as a way of "defending their right to life."[49] These statistics indicate that the poor retain a marked degree of cultural and religious autonomy, which the dominant sector is incapable of totally manipulating or understanding. Certain aspects of their cultural and religious life are clearly charged with anti-hegemonic qualities. In complex and ever-changing ways, they sustain an alternative vision of history and society.

Culture, Religion, and Conscientization

Gutiérrez insists that for any process of liberative praxis "to be authentic and complete, it has to be undertaken by the oppressed people themselves and so must stem from the values proper to these people."[50] As we have seen, however, these values are expressed through cultural and religious media that exhibit both positive and negative characteristics. Although they provide oppressed peoples with a certain shelter and autonomy, they sometimes help perpetrate the exploitation they suffer. The challenge is to find some means whereby the poor can better understand the complex characteristics of their own "partially penetrated" culture and beliefs, affirm what is liberating in them and reject what is oppressive. In Gutiérrez's terms, a process must be set in motion whereby the oppressed person "rejects the oppressive consciousness which dwells in him, becomes aware of his situation, and finds his own language."[51] What is required is a social analysis that allows the poor to see the relationship between their culture, religious beliefs, and social position. To facilitate this process he turns to the ideas of Paulo Freire, one of Latin America's foremost educators and cultural analysts.

From this point of view, one of the most creative and fruitful efforts which has been implemented in Latin America is the experimental work of Paulo Freire, who has sought to establish a "pedagogy of the oppressed." By means of an unalienating and liberating "cultural action," which links theory with praxis, the oppressed person perceives — and modifies — his relationship with the world and with other people. He thus makes the transfer from a "naive awareness" which does not deal with problems, gives too much value to the past, tends to accept mythical explanations, and tends toward debate — to a "critical awareness" — which delves into problems, is open to new ideas, replaces magical explanations with real causes, and tends to dialogue.[52]

In condensed terms, Freire's pedagogy attempts to develop a type of total literacy that goes beyond the written word and includes an articulate personal awareness of how society works. The conscientization process is carefully designed not to reject totally the "partially penetrated" consciousness of the oppressed, but rather uses it as the initial phoneme on which an increasingly critical and realistic language is built. The protest pent up in the poor along with their repressed vision of a different social order are accordingly articulated on the basis of their own experience and words.

When the oppressed begin to perceive their place in society and history in a more conscious and critical way, culture and religion assume a more dynamic and challenging role in their lives. Instead of being "channels used to inject the ideology of the dominant sector in accord with their own interests,"[53] they serve to orientate them in the project of liberation. As critically appropriated expressions of self-understanding and hope in the future, they provide the poor with the self-knowledge and spiritual motivation necessary for political action and ultimate liberation. Gutiérrez states time and again that radical social transformation is possible only if the poor achieve a deep sense of their own lives and an appreciation of their role in the evolution of human history. These qualities are indispensable if liberative praxis is to avoid the trap of self-defeating superficiality and ultimate cynicism.

What Gutiérrez proposes is a reappropriation of popular culture and religion by the poor themselves. When they become conscious of themselves as an oppressed social group and develop the socio-political literacy necessary for effective action, they can repossess their culture and religious beliefs freed from the distortion of the dominant sector's ideology. Kudó describes this process in almost lyrical terms:

We can speak then . . . of a new popular culture, that is to say, of a new way of living, producing, acting, feeling, thinking, organizing, singing, and dancing that fundamentally appears as a rejection and protest against the culture or ideology of the dominant class to the extent that it reflects the real interests and collective will of the exploited classes.[54]

These words are not based solely on conjecture and wishful thinking. Both Kudó and Gutiérrez have worked in *comunidades de base* where people have striven to reappropriate critically their cultural and religious heritage. The results are as dynamic as Kudó's words. These basic and powerful social forces have been reconverted and reinvested as vital ingredients in the liberative and utopic efforts of the oppressed to establish a radically transformed world. They have become a source of a "deideologized" self-expression and the basis of a revolutionary spirituality that is actively shaping the Peruvian political process and Christian community.

Culture, Religion, and the Remaking of History

The attitude of Gutiérrez and his associates toward culture and religion transcends the often crass posture of both the extreme right and left of the Peruvian political spectrum. The former views culture and religion as ideological tools to be used in manipulating the masses, while the latter sees them as so many indices of backwardness and alienation. For Gutiérrez and the members of the Las Casas team, however, culture and religion are key ingredients in the struggle for social change. They are indispensable forms of self-expression that vitalize and sustain people in the struggle for liberation. As Vidales and Kudó note, the conscientization process, or *toma de conciencia*,[55] aims at helping the poor reappropriate the radical potential of their culture and belief. By achieving an autonomous sense of self the poor radicalize their Christian faith and remove the dross of passive religiosity.

> To the extent that the popular classes that identify themselves as Christian . . . enter, assume, and live out their religious practices within and in dialectical relation to the process of liberation (conscientization, politicization, organization and mobilization, progressive and effective participation in processes of social decision making, etc.), they recover religion's potential for protest (utopia), which assumes an active role and effectively contributes to the process of revolutionary social transformation.[56]

Vidales and Kudó point out that there are two related steps in this process of grassroots analysis and reappropriation:

> This process implies a double task: a reactivation, unblocking, unmasking, and denunciation. That is to say, it requires a critical examination in terms of the religious practices of the exploited classes as well as conscientization, creativity, and transformative living. In

this terrain lies the pedagogical and organization task that makes real and effective advances possible.[57]

There are two vital ingredients necessary in the process described: leaders and effective organizational structures. Among the poor are people with charisms of self-awareness, integrity, and a will to political change. These men and women have to act as "organic intellectuals,"[58] who express and synthesize the hopes of their own people. They are committed to the cause of their oppressed sisters and brothers, not as a revolutionary elite, but as persons of and for the poor. Theirs is a vital ministry of political and ecclesial service. Gifted with a special feel for their fellows, they help structure an articulate agenda for social action. In short, they are grassroots organizers. Gutiérrez and the members of his team have learned from experience that without such people the processes of conscientization and social change will invariably flounder. For this reason they devote a great deal of their time in the *pueblos jovenes* to leadership training, which includes both socio-political analysis and theological education.

The challenge for the "organic intellectual" and conscienticized poor is to tap the power of their culture and belief in such a way that they point to "the urgency of a revolutionary process"[59] and stimulate appropriate socio-political action on its behalf. This train of thought is not unique to the members of the Las Casas team. As they mention, it is rooted in the ideas of Mariátegui and Gramsci, who were convinced that effective social change must arise from the hope-filled consciousness and political will of the oppressed themselves.

> When we speak of the utopic element...we are speaking of what Mariátegui calls "myth," which means a force that moves men in history: "Without myth human existence has no meaning," as Mariátegui says. Therefore, we attribute to the notion of utopia a dynamic and historic weight, that is to say, a "revolutionary" weight according to the Marxist tradition developed especially by Gramsci and ascribed to by Mariátegui.[60]

Once they are critically reappropriated, culture and religion act as "myths" or "utopic mobilizers" that serve to "nourish, sustain, and dynamize historical action." They provide the models and motivation for the construction of a different social order, that is, a different history and vision of society.

Gutiérrez is a keen student of history, not the official textbook version of the dominant class, but that of the poor, which resides in their memory. Having assimilated many ideas from Ernst Bloch, a Marxist philosopher who devoted his life to studying the revolutionary potential of oppressed peoples' culture and beliefs, Gutiérrez is aware that these social phenomena can serve as templates or symbols for utopia. He sees utopia as a powerful vision of futurity, a dream of newness and liberation that resides in the historical experience of the poor. In events and persons such as Francis of Assisi, the peasant war lead by Thomas Münzer, and the struggle of Bartolomé de Las Casas for social justice in colonial Latin America, he perceives "oases" of resistance that challenged the social values and religious assumptions of their day.

What are often erroneously described as mere cultural and "spiritual movements of the poor" were "frequently social movements as well,"[61] whose finality was to change the course of history. The poverty of Francis, the egalitarian, Christian society of Münzer, and the writings of Las Casas all stemmed in varying degrees from a utopic, revolutionary vision of society. Although the dominant sector has tried to either obliterate the "dangerous" memory of these events and persons or distort and neutralize them with its ideological and class-related version of history, they prove that the hopes of the poor are never totally extinguished by oppression.

In Latin America indigenous groups that have been portrayed as totally malleable in the hands of the dominant sector have shown an ability to challenge the power and assumption of their oppressors. Their resistance has often coalesced around traditional Christian symbols of freedom and salvation.

> From the beginning of the conquest, the indigenous peoples of America revolted against their oppressors. The written history speaks very little of this. However, gradually, we have recuperated the memory of the struggles for liberation in the continent. As time has passed, Christian motives have become present in these rebellions. The Indians who received the gospel found in it reasons for rejecting the oppression to which they were being submitted. They interpreted the gospel from their own situation and from their own culture.[62]

Although Spanish court theologians debated whether they were truly human and possessed souls, indigenous peoples were capable of perceiving an underlying demand for social justice in the otherwise distorted faith that was imposed on them. As Gutiérrez mentions, they interpreted and appropriated Christianity in light of their own experience and needs and found in it motives and sustenance in a long series of rebellions that stretched over four centuries. In many ways basic Christian communities are carrying on that same tradition at the present moment.

Gutiérrez is convinced that the memory of innumerable struggles carried on by the "scourged Christs of America" continues to challenge the prevailing order as a model of subversion and resistance often evident in seemingly innocuous "cultural and religious expressions." The memory of these struggles calls for a rereading of history, not from the perspective of the dominant sector, but from the viewpoint of the poor who gave their lives for a different vision of history and society.

Rereading history means remaking history. It means repairing it from the bottom up. And so it will be a subversive history. History must be turned upside-down from the bottom, not from the top.[63]

Rereading the subversive history of the oppressed is not a question of "reassuring nostalgia and pleasant reveries." It is, rather, a question of seeing the vital connection "between the struggles of today and yesterday." Rereading history means recognizing that in the memories and present experience of the poor there is a vital strain of subversion, a subterranean current that can erode the power of oppression. Given sufficient time and spokespersons willing to struggle for its realization, it has "the capability of overcoming every obstacle, even repression itself."[64]

Conscientization also affects the way those poor who are explicitly Christian understand their faith. It ceases to be something "received" and taken for granted, becoming instead an informed, more vital commitment to full liberation. The faith-life of these people draws its vitality from the subversive, anti-hegemonic strain that runs through Scripture. The experience of the Exodus and Jesus' critique of the religious and political oppressors of his time become motifs that energize the Christian's self-understanding and action in society. In Gutiérrez words:

> Christians have the right to think through their faith in the Lord, to think out the experience of their own liberation. They have the right to reclaim their faith — a faith that is continually diverted away from their experience of being poor — in order to turn it into an ideological exposé of the situation of domination that makes and keeps them poor.[65]

What is called for is a reappropriation of faith and the Bible that must be reread "militantly," that is, "in solidarity with the struggles of the poor." This prevents "the private proprietors of the world's goods from being the private proprietors of the word of the Lord as well,"[66] thus converting it into an ideological sham. Faith becomes something subversive. It criticizes oppressors and announces the real possibility of social change, of a fuller humanity consonant with the demands of Scripture. It is not the possession of an institution, but the spirit and action of people struggling for liberation.

When Gutiérrez speaks of rereading and rewriting history, he means understanding it as a vital expression of the lives of oppressed peoples. History is not a mere theoretical concept. It is, rather, an expression of our human creativity, something we "do" and "make." Rereading and rewriting history from the "bottom up" implies coming to terms with the humanity and creativity of the poor. As a Christian, Gutiérrez also believes that their lives speak of a God present in history, a God who directs them to ultimate liberation.

It is necessary to insist that history (where God reveals himself and

where we preach him) must be interpreted from the viewpoint of the
poor, "the condemned of the earth." Human history has been written
"by a white hand" from the dominating sectors. A clear example of
this is the history of our continent and of our country, Peru. The
perspective of the "defeated" of history is different. Efforts have been
made to wipe from their own minds the memory of their struggles.
This is to deprive them of a source of energy, of historical will of
rebellion.

Christianity as it has been historically lived has been, and is,
closely tied to a culture: Western; to a race: the white race; to a
class: the dominant class. Its history has also been written by a
white, western, and bourgeois hand. We must regain the memory of
the "beaten Christs of the Indies" as Bartolomé de Las Casas called
the Indians of the American continent.[67]

The history of the poor differs radically from that of the dominant
sector, for it is one of exploitation and hope, not domination and the maintenance of class power. It does not live in the established version of history
but in the culture and beliefs that sustain the poor in their oppression.
Likewise, the God of the poor is not that of the ruling class, their divinized
self-image that sanctions and guarantees their power. Their God is rather
the one who offers hope and stands by them in the struggle for justice.

Gutiérrez is convinced that throughout "history there has been a repressed but resurgent theology" evident in oppressed peoples' struggle for
a more just social order. Although this theology is "expressed in tenta-
tive formulations, hence in formulations not immune to impatience and
ambiguity,"[68] there is no doubt in his mind that it differs radically from
the theology of the dominant class. It is a theology that speaks of social equality and effective justice as the foundation of faith in God rather
than one grounded in abstract and ahistorical principles. The challenge for
the Christian, especially as an "organic intellectual," is to articulate and
strengthen the revolutionary potential of this inchoate theology and make
it the spiritual foundation for liberative praxis. Thus, theology becomes a
source of subversion rather than "superversion," which sanctifies the status
quo.

We are not faced here with new fields of application of old theological
notions, but with the provocation and necessity to live and think
the faith in different socio-cultural categories. This has occurred at
other times in the history of the Christian community and has always
produced fears and anxieties. In this search, we are impelled by the
urgency to pronounce the Word of the Lord in our everyday language.

This is the point at issue; a rereading of the Gospel message from
the standpoint of liberating practice. Theological discourse operates
here as a mediator between a new manner of living the faith, and

its communication. If we accept that theology is a re-reading of the Gospel, this is carried out with a view to the proclamation of the message.[69]

What Gutiérrez describes is a reshaping of theology in such a way that it coincides with the "cultural universe"[70] of the poor. He is speaking of a "distinct theological perspective [that] comes from the social practice of the true Latin American people."[71] It critically employs their values and beliefs rather than the ideology of the dominant sector. Such a process does not result in fixed theological formulations. They are, rather, subject to constant reinterpretation. What Gutiérrez proposes is an on-going rewriting of faith and theology that incorporates current experiences of the "evangelical message... along with the experiences it has brought about throughout history."[72] In this way they recapitulate and express what was and is most utopic in the struggle of the poor for a liberated world.

Analysis

The approach of Gutiérrez and his associates in the Las Casas Center to the culture and religious life of the poor is complex, and we need to summarize and assess it in some way. Their position is solid, grounded on thorough study and personal experience of the poor as people. Given the general complexity of culture and religion, however, it is impossible that anyone should formulate a totally satisfactory, all-encompassing explanation of their social role. Fortunately there is a wealth of material written by other social theorists that can fill out certain lacunae in the material we have been considering. In the paragraphs that follow we shall reiterate the main points of the Las Casas team's position and relate them to the insights of other scholars.

According to Gutiérrez and his colleagues, whether culture and religion play a negative or positive role in the process of liberation depends on a number of variables. In theological language, culture and religion can be either sinful or salvific forces depending on who uses them and for what ends. In the social sciences scholars often speak of the ideological or utopic power of culture and religion. Gutiérrez is familiar with the long and complex discussion that has gone on in the social sciences about the nature and role of ideology and utopia and how they affect our social behavior.[73] As we have seen, both concepts surface in his writings and are discussed at length in *A Theology of Liberation*.[74] He also uses the terms adjectivally when he speaks of the "ideological" and "utopic" characteristics of the culture and religion of the poor. Precisely what does Gutiérrez mean by these terms?

Gutiérrez views ideology as a multifaceted process whereby the self-understanding and class-related interests of a minority are officially propagated and enforced as a social norm with oppressive and ultimately sinful effects. The key concept to keep in mind here is "process." Ideology, like utopia, is neither a mere mental abstraction nor some sort of object. It is, rather, a set of values specific to a certain class of people that shapes their social action. It molds their assumptions about life and influences their behavior. In a class stratified society like that of Peru, the dominant elite is convinced that the capitalist system it lives from is inherently superior. Given its obvious power, this group of people attempts to control society in ways that coincide with its interests, despite the fact that such interests produce more misery than well-being for the majority of the population. Convinced of the logic and superiority of capitalism, the rich blithely over-look its consequences. Their beliefs, then, are ideological. Their culture and even religious practices reinforce their assumptions and are likewise ideological.

Gutiérrez is aware, however, that the impact of the dominant sector's ideological assumptions and actions is never total. Although the oppressed sector's culture and religion are "partially penetrated" by ideological val-ues of capitalism, the poor never totally lose their sense of uniqueness nor surrender their hope for a more just society. This sense of autonomous selfhood and hope is the basic ingredient of utopia, a complex force that counterbalances the weight of ideological oppression. Utopia is an expres-sion of that which is not yet but is in the process of becoming. It is voiced in song and poetry, political action and the struggle for justice. It may seem an ephemeral and unreal symbol, but actually it galvanizes the imagination of the poor and sustains them in the struggle for liberation.

Gutiérrez understands ideology and utopia as characteristics of social behavior that cannot be understood outside of the "social classes that con-stitute their historical subject."[75] By focusing on the subjects who embody ideological and utopic processes, Gutiérrez avoids the danger of treating them as mere things or static qualities of social behavior that can some-how be isolated and defined apart from peoples' lives. His views coincide with those of a number of social scientists who stress the subjective and dynamic qualities of the processes in question. As John Thompson points out, ideology cannot be treated as something external and objectifiable since, like utopia, it is an internal and inter-subjective social force.

> Ideology cannot be treated as a mere "thing-out-there" to be observed and investigated empirically, for it necessarily points back to the prob-lematic of self-understanding and calls for ... [a] sort of reflexive social theory.[76]

Gutiérrez is in agreement with Thompson's insights to the extent that his first concern is that the subjects of ideology and utopia understand themselves and their role in society. He insists on conscientization as a necessary first step in the liberation of the poor; this provides them with the "reflexive social theory" Thompson calls for. Conscientization forces them to come to terms with the various forces that shape their values and actions. It makes them stand back, as it were, and critically analyze how their social identity has been molded and has made them who they are. At the same time they see the necessity of developing an autonomous, utopic vision that corresponds to their own experience as oppressed peoples.

What really concerns Gutiérrez is that people consciously come to terms with the ideological and utopic forces in their lives. He focuses accordingly on the social role of these concepts rather than on what they mean abstractly. In his analysis of the meaning of hegemony in Gramsci's writings, Raymond Williams, a British literary critic and social philosopher, offers a description of this concept that coincides well with Gutiérrez's understanding of ideology and utopia. Neither is perceived as an objectifiable "system or a structure," but rather as "a realized complex of experiences, relationships, and activities, with specific and changing pressures and limits."[77] To varying degrees they influence the way we act as social beings. For this very reason ideology and utopia defy simple, unchanging definition.

In accord with a number of other social analysts, Gutiérrez sees ideology as a type of "cognitive filter" that limits a society's self-definition and purpose for the sake of "a determinate situation system"[78]—that of the dominant sector. Yet he does not lose sight of the fact that ideology has palpable consequences for its victims. As he emphatically points out, the capitalist ideology of Latin America's elites is more than a flawed set of values or a sort of innocuous social myopia. It is, rather, a type of convenient blindness — a sin of omission in theological terms — in which those who so ardently believe in the dominant system's values "fail" to see the effects of the very system they espouse and benefit from.

In Gutiérrez's own words, "ideology does not offer adequate and scientific knowledge of reality; rather it masks it."[79] Sealed off from the negative effects of its values and actions, the dominant sector, with its partial and self-serving definition of life, inflicts immense suffering on millions of people. Wittingly or not, elites live off oppression and injustice. In perhaps his most succinct analysis of the effects of capitalism as an ideological system, Gutiérrez speaks of a continent of "non-persons" — people "considered less than human by society, because that society is based on privileges arrogated by a minority."[80] More accurately, however, it is not "society" that perceives the poor as "non-persons," but a minority whose ideological values allow it to disregard the humanity of the majority.

In his varied treatments of ideology and utopia, oppression and resistance, Gutiérrez describes what are ultimately theological issues. As we have seen repeatedly, ideological and utopic forces also affect peoples' beliefs and behavior, and these facets of social existence have clear theological ramifications. Without making simplistic equations, Gutiérrez often describes ideology as a type of social sin and utopia as a foreshadowing of the reign of God. In a poignant description of sin, Gutiérrez describes a

theological phenomenon that is remarkably similar to his understanding of
the sociological effects of ideology.

Sin is found in the refusal to accept any person as a neighbor, in
oppressive structures built up for the benefit of the few, in the despo-
liation of peoples, races, cultures, and social classes. Sin is basically
an alienation, and as such, it cannot be found floating in the air, but
is found in concrete historical situations, in individual and specific
alienations. It is impossible to understand one without the other.[81]

Utopia, on the other hand, is a vehicle of "creative imagination"[82] which
leads to the "construction of a society which functions for the poor."[83]
It opens the way for a *"praxis of love"*[84] in which the human potential
of all people can come to term in accord with God's plan for creation.
Thus, we see the clear link between the social and theological in Gutiérrez's
writings. His appreciation of the destructive effects of ideology informs his
understanding of sin. Likewise, the utopic struggle of oppressed peoples
for liberation shapes his understanding of salvation.

In *We Drink from Our Own Wells,* Gutiérrez characterizes the social
life of Latin America as a struggle between ideological and utopic forces,
between sin and salvation. As only a theologian could, he refers to the
present historical moment in Latin America as "a time of solidarity and a
time of prayer — but also, and in a sense synthesizing the two, a time of
martyrdom."[85] The martyrdom is fundamentally the result of the dominant
class's resistance to a new vision of society. In theological terms, it is a
reflection of their unwillingness to accept the dignity of the poor as co-heirs
in the process of creation with the same dignity and rights they possess. As
Gutiérrez knows full well, this refusal has assumed a particularly virulent
and violent form on his own continent. Nonetheless, he sees the difficulties
of the present as adding "up to a time of salvation and judgment, a time
of grace and stern demand — a time above all of hope."[86] These are the
words not only of a theologian but of a poet and mystic who can look at
his own people in their present oppression and see a glimmer of light in
their lives despite what they now endure.

Toward a Fuller Picture

As one reads Gutiérrez's works it becomes increasingly clear that he views
the struggle between the ideological forces and the utopic forces in society as a contest about the meaning of history. He describes a process of
constant social friction in which two opposing groups, the oppressors and
the oppressed, vie with each other about the shape and finality of their
world. To use a term drawn from Alain Touraine, the rich and the poor
are engaged in a battle about "historicity." The term "historicity" refers
to the process whereby social classes struggle to establish their particu-

lar "formation of meaning" and *a system of orientation of conduct*"[87] as norms.

Without denying the basic antithesis between the rich and poor, we should keep in mind that there is constant interplay between the two groups in the events of daily existence. Obviously, the poor are caught up in a struggle for survival. Simply feeding themselves and their children is an immense challenge. Oppressed peoples are forced to contend with daily injustice and socio-political oppression. They must learn how to respond to the dominant system and either accept it as an inevitable fact of life or somehow struggle against it. Many decide to come to terms with the status quo. As Gutiérrez points out, there is both fear and passivity among oppressed peoples as well as resistance. It is equally obvious that the dominant sector, at least more often than not, does not *consciously* set out to exploit the poor.

These factors must be taken into account if any analysis, including that of Gutiérrez, is to avoid the trap of viewing class struggle as a type of battle with clearly defined lines. All too often they are difficult to delineate. On occasion Gutiérrez and his associates in the Las Casas Center are prone to describe class struggle as if it were a question of two antagonistic, irreconcilable social groups. They make few references to the middle class and the role they play as mediators of the dominant sector's ideological values. This fact, along with the overly Lima-orientated focus of Gutiérrez and the Las Casas team, are two of the more problematic aspects of their presentation. What we propose now is to find a way of overcoming these limitations. A number of North American and European theorists provide ideas that fill in the gaps.

In the Peruvian context the middle class plays a crucial socio-political role by "buffering" the extreme disparity between the rich and poor. Furthermore, because the vast majority of teachers and members of the military come from middle-class backgrounds, they have the most direct contact with the poor through compulsory schooling and the draft. To the extent that they subscribe to the values of capitalism, and most do, they act as the primary mediators of its ideological messages.

In Peru the rich and middle classes, who form a small minority of the population, dominate the state, control its socio-economic assets, and disseminate the ideology of capitalism. Bound together by tacit and ever-changing political alliances, they use the educational, mass media, and even religious institutions in their control to shape what Geertz calls the "symbolic templates" and "suasive images"[88] that directly affect a society's self-definition and, most importantly, mode of reproduction. As Marshall Sahlins puts it in *Culture and Practical Reason,* their values and actions help create and sustain a "classificatory grid"[89] that defines what is acceptable or unacceptable socio-economic and political activity.

In short, they advocate and direct "a definite form of cultural order; or a cultural order acting in a particular form,"[90] namely, that of contemporary capitalism. Unfortunately, Gutiérrez rarely refers to the various social strata in Peru and other Third World countries. He spends little time analyzing how dominant and what might be called "subdominant" social groups interrelate and forge alliances. He generally speaks only of the rich and poor, oppressors and oppressed. This antithetical type of language is not entirely invalid, but it can unintentionally leave readers with simplistic notions about inter-class relations and the way ideological penetration is affected.

The power of the "suasive images" Geertz refers to must not be underestimated. They are inculcated through schooling, nationalistic propaganda, and religious training, which, despite their different emphases, all speak of the normalcy and naturalness of the status quo. As Paul Willis notes in his study of working-class youths in British society exposed to a constant barrage of ideological messages, they come to accept the inherently relative values of the dominant class as normative and benign despite the fact that this acceptance weakens their class solidarity and political will, thus relegating them to chronic poverty. This process clearly goes on in Peru as well, albeit in distinct forms. In Willis's words:

> One of the most important general functions of ideology is the way in which it turns uncertain and fragile cultural resolutions and outcomes into a pervasive naturalism.[91]

The shared presuppositions about the way society should and does function that ideological processes help create often serve as a type of inter-class cement. The less aware working-class people are of their uniqueness and the causes of their socio-economic marginalization, the easier it is to guarantee "uncoerced outcomes which have the function of maintaining the structure of society and the status quo."[92]

As Willis notes with poignancy, when ideological apparatuses are truly effective, the working class ultimately is condemned to a type of self-damnation evident in passivity and self-destructive behavior.[93] As we saw in the Las Casas Center's analysis of the socio-religious beliefs of students and independent workers in Lima, Willis's point is well taken. Generally more exposed to the ideology of capitalism, they display the highest tolerance of the status quo and are the most prone to believe uncritically in its values. As Michael Mann points out, these peoples have come to internalize "the moral expectations of the ruling class" and accept their "own inferior position as legitimate."[94] Thus they unwittingly perpetuate a social system that is antithetical to their real human development and freedom. Not surprisingly, their belief in individual effort and trust in the current social system make them the most apolitical members of Lima's working class.

As well as cultivating conformity, ideological apparatuses and the people involved in them actively counteract and subvert the efforts of oppressed peoples to achieve critical self- and political awareness. But they generally do this in subtle and convoluted ways. Gutiérrez often refers to the overt violence directed against the popular movement, but this is more the exception than the rule. Ideological apparatuses first attempt to erode the class consciousness of oppressed peoples, since violence can often "backfire" and produce class solidarity among its victims.

As Willis found in his analysis of the most "rebellious" adolescents in British trade schools, administrators were adept at capitalizing on their very rebelliousness. By singling out the most articulate students and subjecting them to a mix of punishment and praise, they arrested the development of a more adequate and systematic critique of the school system, which pounds the ethos of capitalism into their heads. A type of passive-aggressive behavior was deliberately cultivated among working-class boys, which effectively neutralized the growth of further socio-political and class consciousness.

> For our purposes, the two most important "downward" vertical impacts of ideology on the counter-school culture are those of confirmation and dislocation. They confirm (in a somewhat circular fashion) those aspects and resolutions of cultural processes which are most partial to the current social organization of interest and production, and dislocate (bringing something new into the local system) those which retain a degree of critical penetration of that system.[95]

In a country like Peru a similar process underlies the constant efforts of the government to bring "rebellious" social groups into line. Labor unions, political parties, and even segments of the church are alternately excoriated as subversive and invited to enter into "dialogue" with members of the government.

In what is often a Machiavellian scenario, the leaders of the dominant sector attempt to erode the credibility of the popular movement by assuaging the people involved in it with promises of cooperation and substantive change in order to tame their militancy. The few changes that come about, of course, are almost always cosmetic and leave the ideological values and apparatuses of the dominant sector intact. As Gutiérrez mentions in something of an understatement, maintaining the integrity and vision of the popular movement in such a situation requires "an appreciable degree of political maturity."[96]

Our analysis of certain "gaps" in Gutiérrez's understanding of ideology and utopia requires qualification. First, and most importantly, our criticism is not meant as an attack on the integrity or theoretical adequacy of his approach. He describes the lives of people in Lima's *pueblos jovenes* in accurate detail and backs up his descriptions with an array of well chosen social scientific information adeptly woven into his presentation. As we have intimated, however, he pays insufficient attention to class interaction and the ways in which the "partial ideological penetration" of the poor is affected.

It must be kept in mind that the popular movement is a relatively new force in Peru. Its members constantly struggle to understand adequately and counteract the "partial penetration" that affects them as well as the majority of the population. Furthermore, the question of the popular movement's relation to the middle class has yet to be resolved. While some of its members call for confrontation, others prefer to win over the middle class to the cause of the poor. These delicate questions of the popular movement's self-identity and strategies have yet to be solved. Conscious of these complex issues and aware that they can be resolved only with sufficient time and experience, Gutiérrez prefers subtle criticism of the popular movement's problems to negative analysis. Although his critique is couched, it is present in his works. A careful analysis of his writings, particularly the notes, provides references to many of the Latin American popular movement's problems as well as proposed remedies.

Importance of "Fissures"

Given the all-pervasiveness of the capitalist system in Latin America, Gutiérrez's constant assertion that its oppressive effects "can and must be transformed by the action of the people"[97] may seem like wishful thinking. Yet the power of the capitalist sector and the ideological values it espouses are always subject to challenge. According to the noted social theorist Jürgen Habermas, the advocates of capitalism put much credence in the "logic of scientific-technical progress," which supposedly rules the "free market" with a "law-like character."[98] "Progress" is said to be an inevitable product of capital accumulation, a blessing to which all are called. The beneficent deity of commerce, however, can be most capricious. Precipitous drops in petroleum and metal prices at the present moment are a case in point. Such shifts, however, are not necessarily bad. If the economic power of the ruling class diminishes so can the effectiveness of its ideological processes. Thus, Gutiérrez's belief in the possibility of the poor's utopic hope affecting social change is not unfounded. It is not mere optimism that leads him to this conclusion, but rather close scrutiny of the interplay between dominant and repressed social classes.

As the studies of the Las Casas Center point out, there are always "fissures" in the ideological values and power of the dominant sector through which "subterranean streams gush up." These form what Gutiérrez calls "oases"[99] in which alternate historicities coalesce. These "cracks" or debilities in ideological processes have also been examined by other social analysts. Michael Mann provides insights into the inherent debilities of any ruling class's ideology that can eventually lead to social criticism and a radical challenge to prevailing social structures:

1. Most general values, norms and social beliefs usually mentioned as integrating societies are extremely vague, and can be used to legitimate any social structure, existing or not.
2. Even if a value is stated precisely, it may lead to conflict, not cohesion. For while some values unite men, others necessarily divide them.
3. The standards embodied in values are absolute ones, and it is difficult for such absolutes to co-exist without conflict. For example, the modern Western values of "achievement" and "equality" ... each limit the scope of the other.[100]

Mann's observations are substantiated by the field work of Vidales and Kudó. As they have demonstrated, the poor of Lima's *pueblos jovenes* often see through the false logic of the dominant sector's values. They are frequently aware that the principles they espouse have nothing to do with the socio-political and economic actions they take.

There are several other potential weaknesses in the dominant sector's hegemonic position that Mann does not mention but Gutiérrez refers to obliquely throughout his writings. Often ideological values can become self-evident and self-satisfying truths that blind the dominant sector to the real basis on which their cultural and political hegemony is built. The distortion their ideology produces can affect them as much as the classes they dominate. Turner spells out how this can happen in *Dramas, Fields and Metaphors:*

The danger is, of course, that the more persuasive the root metaphor or archetype, the more chance it has of becoming a self-certifying myth, sealed off from empirical disproof. It remains a fascinating metaphysics.[101]

"Fascinating metaphysics," however, is inadequate for holding together a class stratified society. When the values of the dominant sector are "sealed off from empirical disproof," they run the risk of becoming truisms incapable of demonstrating their validity to the dominated sector.

These truisms are also capable of doing immense damage to a society's political and economic structures, as has become evident in many national security states. Obsessed with the "metaphysics" of capitalist development, the military and members of the ruling elite have wreaked havoc with their countries' resources and peoples generating systemic poverty and oppression rather than progress. In many Latin American countries this process has lead to a growing criticism of the dominant sector and a resurgence of the popular movement. Thus, we are presented with what appears to be an enigmatic datum: under certain circumstances the more self-assured the dominant sector becomes the more prone it is to arrogance and mistakes that elicit resistance.

There is also the danger that the "self-certifying" myths of the dominant class will prevent it from understanding the real character of those it dominates. The ruling class faction can inadequately assess the residual cohesion and independence of the poor because of the myopia their own culture induces. As Raymond Williams points out in *Marxism and Literature*, the ideological processes the dominant class utilizes to buoy up their hegemonic position can "discard whole areas of significance . . . or convert them into forms which . . . do not contradict"[102] its perception of things, but this does not mean they cease to exist.

In a country like Peru, where the difference between the rich and poor is cultural as well as economic, the selective vision of the dominant class can diminish the reach and effectiveness of ideological processes. National elites consider the culture of workers and *campesinos* as an embarrassing residue from a bygone age of underdevelopment. As Gutiérrez mentions in terms of popular religiosity, it "is something beyond the comprehension, and beneath the contempt, of the 'enlightened' bourgeois mentality."[103] But the dominant sector ignores this and other aspects of popular culture to the peril of its ideological hegemony. To the extent that the poor become aware of their real place in society and the causes of their oppression, an autonomous culture, language, and religiosity have the potential of becoming powerful symbols and "sources of dialectical opposition to the bourgeois ideology and dominant culture."[104]

Gutiérrez's contention that the poor are capable of forming a cohesive socio-political body that challenges the hegemony of the dominant sector is substantiated by the ideas of Victor Turner, who, as an anthropologist, has studied the dynamics of inter-class relations in several Third World countries. According to Turner, despite the monolithic appearance of the ruling class's social program and the seeming invincibility of its power, they are part of what he calls "a socio-cultural 'field' in which many options are provided." If the popular movement can achieve sufficient internal cohesion and an adequate strategy for change, the power of the dominant sector "can be undermined and multiple alternative programs may be generated."[105]

In many ways what Gutiérrez calls the popular movement is related to what Turner describes as "communitas": an "antistructural, . . . undifferentiated, equalitarian, direct, nonrational (though not *ir*rational)"[106] social framework. "Communitas" challenges the ideological processes of the dominant class by creating and affirming autonomous "root metaphors, conceptual archetypes, [and] paradigms"[107] that contradict those of the dominant class. The exact shape these forms of opposition will take, if any, depends on the ability of the dominated class to articulate them and the hegemonic sector's ability to cope with and repress them. As we shall see in the sixth chapter, Gutiérrez sees the popular church that has emerged in Latin America as one of the prime examples of "communitas" and bearer of utopic hope. It is precisely for this reason that he devotes so much of his personal time and energy to its development.

As we have noted, Gutiérrez is convinced that the only effective means for overcoming the oppressive effects of the dominant sector's ideological control and oppression is by finding the means of opposition in the life experiences and culture of the poor. There is a great deal of wisdom in such a position. His insights, however, could be strengthened by a broader analysis of his country's own socio-cultural makeup. A more inclusive analysis of the culture of ordinary Peruvians is all the more imperative at the present moment because of a complex political phenomenon known as *Sendero Luminoso* or, in English, the *Shining Path*. In the most condensed of terms, *Sendero Luminoso* is a guerrilla movement that originated in the province of Ayacucho in the central Andes and has now spread to most parts of the country. It is a political phenomenon without parallel in Latin America; few people understand it because of its highly secretive infrastructure. It publishes nothing, working rather by word of mouth.

Sendero Luminoso clearly draws on the frustration and cultural marginalization of people in the Peruvian *sierra* as well as urban immigrants. *Sendero Luminoso* has enticed many *campesinos* and workers into its ranks by preaching a revindication of indigenous rights mixed with an eclectic type of Maoist philosophy. It speaks of a new social order, but it has created something destructive rather than hope-filled and utopic. Drawing heavily on the resentment of the poor, it offers them an opportunity to vent their feelings on those who oppress them, particularly wealthy landowners and the police. It is an intriguing but tragic case of a segment of the popular movement that has tried to vindicate the oppression of the poor by violence, only to produce greater suffering and oppression for those whom it promises to liberate. What *Sendero Luminoso* demonstrates all too graphically is that without a utopic vision of justice and human dignity, along with criteria for measuring its own compliance with these values, the popular movement runs the risk of going radically astray. Its power is a two-edged sword whose destructive qualities are as sharp as its constructive potential.

Gutiérrez is fully aware of this. It is precisely for this reason that he stresses the need for self-analysis among the oppressed. They must constantly take stock of their lives and values. Their political action must be gauged in terms of a vision of liberation. A process of on-going conscientization is indispensable if aberrations like *Sendero Luminoso* are to be avoided. The Las Casas Center study of culture and religious practices in the *pueblos jovenes* is one step among many in the task of the poor to achieve critical self-consciousness. The information it provides is not meant to grace book shelves, but to be returned and synthesized by the people who are its subjects. It is a study of the symbols and rituals, pathos and passion that sustain the poor in their struggle for liberation.

NOTES

1. As quoted in Gutiérrez, *We Drink from Our Own Wells: The Spiritual Journey of a People,* trans. Matthew J. O'Connell (Maryknoll, N.Y.: Orbis Books; Melbourne, Australia: Dove Communications, 1983), p. 156.
2. José María Arguedas, "La novela y el problema de la expresión literaria en el Perú," in *Yawar Fiesta* (Santiago: Editorial Universitaria, 1973), p. 17.
3. See Gutiérrez, *A Theology of Liberation: History, Politics and Salvation,* trans. and ed. Sister Caridad Inda and John Eagleson (Maryknoll, N.Y.: Orbis Books, 1973), pp. 74–75.
4. Gutiérrez, *The Power of the Poor in History: Selected Works,* trans. Robert R. Barr (Maryknoll, N.Y.: Orbis Books, 1983), p. 218, note 53.
5. Ibid., p. 97.
6. Jeffrey Klaiber, *Religión y revolución en el Perú 1824–1976* (Lima: Universidad del Pacífico, 1980), p. 130.
7. Gutiérrez understands the "structural-functionalist" tradition to be one characterized by an excessively linear approach to social reality, be it economic or cultural. See *A Theology of Liberation,* p. 82.
8. Edward Schillebeeckx, *Christ: The Experience of Jesus as Lord* (New York: Seabury Press, 1980), p. 58.
9. Tokihiro Kudó, *Práctica religiosa y proyecto histórico II: estudio sobre la religiosidad popular en dos barrios de Lima* (Lima: Centro de Estudios y Publicaciones, 1980), p. 9.
10. Gutiérrez, *The Power of the Poor,* pp. 123–124.
11. Kudó, *Práctica religiosa y proyecto histórico II,* pp. 29–30.
12. Tokihiro Kudó, *Hacia una cultura nacional popular* (Lima: Centro de Estudios y Promoción del Desarrollo, 1982), p. 24.
13. Ibid.
14. Ibid., p. 117.
15. Ibid., p. 118.
16. Raúl Vidales and Tokihiro Kudó, *Práctica religiosa y proyecto histórico: hipótesis para un estudio de la religiosidad popular en América Latina* (Lima: Centro de Estudios y Publicaciones, 1975).
17. Gutiérrez, *The Power of the Poor,* p. 193.
18. Vidales and Kudó, p. 116.
19. Ibid.
20. Kudó, *Práctica religiosa y proyecto histórico II,* p. 37.
21. Ibid.
22. Ibid., p. 33.
23. Vidales and Kudó, p. 64.
24. Kudó, *Práctica religiosa y proyecto histórico II,* pp. 193–194.
25. Ibid., p. 174.
26. Kudó, *Hacia una cultura nacional popular,* pp. 22–23.
27. Gutiérrez, *The Power of the Poor,* p. 193.
28. Kudó, *Práctica religiosa y proyecto histórico II,* p. 53.
29. Vidales and Kudó, p. 114.
30. Ibid.
31. Ibid.
32. Ibid., p. 32.
33. Ibid., p. 113.
34. Ibid.
35. Kudó, *Práctica religiosa y proyecto histórico II,* p. 169.
36. Ibid., p. 63.

37. Ibid., p. 130.
38. Vidales and Kudó, p. 71.
39. Ibid.
40. Ibid., p. 111.
41. Kudó, *Práctica religiosa y proyecto histórico II*, p. 83.
42. Ibid., pp. 46–47.
43. Ibid., p. 83.
44. Ibid., p. 123.
45. Ibid.
46. Ibid., p. 85.
47. Ibid.
48. Ibid., pp. 98–99.
49. These statements are taken from Kudó's work *Práctica religiosa y proyecto histórico II,* pp. 105, 106, 149 (twice), and 145 respectively.
50. Gutiérrez, *A Theology of Liberation,* p. 91.
51. Ibid.
52. Ibid.
53. Vidales and Kudó, p. 89.
54. Kudó, *Hacia una cultura nacional popular,* p. 33.
55. The Spanish term *toma de conciencia,* literally "consciousness taking," has far more meaning that its abstract English translation.
56. Vidales and Kudó, p. 114.
57. Ibid., p. 115.
58. The term "organic intellectual" comes from the writings of Antonio Gramsci.
59. Vidales and Kudó, p. 103.
60. Ibid.
61. See Gutiérrez, *The Power of the Poor,* p. 94 and also pp. 202–203.
62. Gutiérrez and Shaull, *Liberation and Change,* ed. Ronald H. Stone (Atlanta: John Knox Press, 1977), p. 75.
63. Gutiérrez, *The Power of the Poor,* p. 21.
64. Ibid., p. 80.
65. Ibid., p. 101.
66. Ibid.
67. Gutiérrez and Shaull, p. 92.
68. Gutiérrez, *The Power of the Poor,* p. 202.
69. Gutiérrez, "Liberation, Theology and Proclamation," in *Concilium* 96, *The Mystical and Political Dimension of the Christian Faith,* ed. Claude Geffré and Gustavo Gutiérrez (New York: Herder and Herder, 1974), p. 71.
70. Ibid., p. 68.
71. Gutiérrez and Shaull, p. 88.
72. Ibid.
73. The classic analysis of these concepts is Karl Mannheim's *Ideology and Utopia: An Introduction to the Sociology of Knowledge.* More recent studies done by anthropologists like Turner and Geertz and neo-Marxist theorists like Williams and Willis provide added depth to Mannheim's seminal work.
74. See Gutiérrez, *A Theology of Liberation,* chap. 11, pp. 213–250.
75. Gutiérrez, *The Power of the Poor,* p. 86.
76. John B. Thompson, "Ideology and Domination," *Canadian Journal of Political and Social Theory,* 7 (Winter/Spring 1983): 171.
77. Raymond Williams, *Marxism and Literature* (Oxford: Oxford University Press, 1977), p. 112.
78. Gutiérrez, *The Power of the Poor,* p. 69.
79. Gutiérrez, *A Theology of Liberation,* p. 235.
80. Gutiérrez, *The Power of the Poor,* p. 92.
81. Gutiérrez and Shaull, p. 84.

82. Gutiérrez, *A Theology of Liberation*, p. 234.
83. Gutiérrez and Shaull, p. 87.
84. Ibid., p. 85.
85. Gutiérrez, *We Drink from Our Own Wells*, p. 22.
86. Ibid., p. 25.
87. Alain Touraine, *The Self-Production of Society*, trans. Derek Coltman (Chicago: University of Chicago Press, 1977), p. 4.
88. Clifford Geertz, *The Interpretation of Cultures: Selected Essays by Clifford Geertz* (New York: Basic Books, 1973), pp. 217, 218.
89. Marshall Sahlins, *Culture and Practical Reason* (Chicago: University of Chicago Press, 1976), p. 211.
90. Ibid., p. 185.
91. Paul E. Willis, *Learning to Labour: How Working Class Kids Get Working Class Jobs* (Westmead, Farnborough, Hampshire: Giwer Publishing Co., 1980), p. 162.
92. Ibid., p. 171.
93. Ibid., p. 175.
94. Michael Mann, "The Social Cohesion of Liberal Democracy," *American Sociological Review* 35 (June 1970): 425.
95. Willis, p. 161.
96. Gutiérrez, *The Power of the Poor*, p. 68.
97. Ibid., p. 81.
98. Jürgen Habermas, "Some Conditions for Revolutionizing Late Capitalist Societies [1968]," in *Canadian Journal of Political and Social Theory* 7 (Winter/Spring) 1983): 35.
99. Gutiérrez, *The Power of the Poor*, p. 202.
100. Mann, 424.
101. Victor Turner, *Dramas, Fields and Metaphors: Symbolic Action and Human Society* (Ithaca: Cornell University Press, 1974), p. 29.
102. Williams, p. 116.
103. Gutiérrez, *The Power of the Poor*, p. 193.
104. Ibid., p. 213.
105. Turner, p. 14.
106. Ibid., pp. 46–47.
107. Ibid., p. 50.

Chapter 3

Gutiérrez's Theology and Peruvian Thought: José María Arguedas and José Carlos Mariátegui

At this juncture the tenor of our discussion will shift. We have looked at Gutiérrez's immediate world on an economic and cultural level. Now we can take stock of the intellectual currents that flow through his writings. Gustavo Gutiérrez is clearly a man "of" and "for" the poor, but he is also a highly qualified scholar whose ideas have been shaped by years of study. Although he would be the last person to mention it, he holds a licentiate in psychology and a doctorate in theology. Gutiérrez studied primarily in Europe, yet no one has influenced his thinking more than two fellow Peruvians: José María Arguedas and José Carlos Mariátegui. Both authors have been cited in previous chapters, but most readers are probably unaware of their crucial place in twentieth-century Peruvian thought. In many ways Arguedas and Mariátegui were Gutiérrez's precursors. Both were writers who struggled to understand their country in terms of the poor. Their ideas and words are part of Peru's intellectual heritage and constantly surface in Gutiérrez's theology giving it a unique pathos and frame of reference.

José María Arguedas

Few people outside of Latin America are familiar with José María Arguedas. Many within the continent, however, consider him one of the greatest novelists of this century. Born to a wealthy *mestizo* family in 1911, his father and stepmother virtually abandoned him in early childhood with the collapse of their marriage. He grew up in closer physical and emotional proximity to the indigenous servants and *colonos* who made up his stepmother's household than he did to his own parents. Through *campesinos* whom his parents despised as "dirty Indians," he learned Quechua and the inner workings of a world few *mestizos* learn exists and fewer come to appreciate. The experience of belonging to two cultures with two distinct languages profoundly shaped his personal development and sense of what it means to be Peruvian.

Arguedas received a doctorate from the University of San Marcos in Lima and eventually became the head of its anthropology department. The professional training he received allowed him to penetrate and categorize the cultural reality of Peru. But his interest in Peruvian culture was more than academic. It was also personal since the worlds of the rich and poor were part of his own self. The dialectical tension between *mestizos* and *campesinos* resided within his own person as much as it did in society at large. A gifted writer, he turned to novels as the most expressive medium for describing Peruvian society and his own pain at being immersed in so much social conflict.

Almost all his novels deal with the conflict between *mestizos* and *campesinos*, the rich and poor. His works are a bilingual and bicultural mix of Quechua and Spanish words and concepts. The history and self-identity of the indigenous Peruvian and the westernized *mestizo* are constantly juxtaposed. As Frances Horning Barraclough points out in the preface to her translation of *Deep Rivers*, Arguedas, more than any Peruvian author, portrays the beauty of the Peruvian landscape, as well as the grimness of social conditions in the Andes, through the eyes of the Indians who are part of it.[1] Among Peruvian writers, he was the first to describe honestly the world of the oppressed from the inside. He sketches the two faces of the country with remarkable realism. One displays despair, class hatred, and an intricate, all-pervasive system of oppression. The other reveals the deep hopes of oppressed people for justice and dignity. These two worlds are not separated but rather intimately bound together as they were in Arguedas's own person.

Arguedas spent his life trying to understand what might be called the correlation of good and evil in the society in which he lived. He was acutely aware of the oppressive effects of *mestizo* culture, and yet he knew many *mestizos* who, as individuals, were essentially decent people caught in a situation of class conflict that they could neither control nor understand. Likewise, he was aware of the pettiness of certain *campesinos* who all too willingly betrayed the interests of their fellows for the sake of personal gain and security. At the same time he was aware of the powerful sense of fellowship among oppressed peoples that he called *la fraternidad de los miserables*, "the fraternity of the miserable."[2] As a child he had heard their hopes expressed in Quechua poetry and song, and he knew there was a strong, redeeming power present in their lives. His novels and poetry are epics of conflict between ideological and utopic forces or, in theological language, between sin and salvation. Unfortunately, little of Arguedas's writing has appeared in English. His constant use of Quechua terms and accented, *campesino* Spanish makes translation extremely difficult.

As well as being masterful literary works, Arguedas's novels are also sociological studies that analyze *la textura social,* or "social fabric," of Peruvian society. He describes the typical attitudes, words, and daily rituals of *campesinos* and urban workers with whom he felt a personal affinity despite his upper-class status. He often juxtaposes their words with those of *mestizos* — the other half of his persona. A good example can be found in *Deep Rivers.* In the narrative that follows Ernesto, an autobiographical figure in Arguedas's novels, listens to the words of a young *mestizo* friend who graphically describes his reaction to the deliberate violence inflicted on the *colonos* of his father's *hacienda:*

> They're always being flogged. My mother suffers for them; but my father has to do his duty. On the big haciendas they tie them to the *pisonay* trees in the courtyards or string them up by the hands to a tree limb and beat them. They have to be beaten. Then they start to weep, along with their wives and children. They don't weep as if they were being punished, but more like orphans do. It's sad. And when you hear them you feel like crying too, the way they do; I used to, brother, when I was a little boy. I don't know what I needed to be consoled about, but I wept as if I were seeking consolation, and not even my mother's arms could comfort me.[3]

Arguedas's powerful description of violence against *campesinos* is neither fiction nor hyperbole. Violence is part of daily life in the Peruvian *sierra,* an ordinary means of social control. And it was the very givenness of such violence that pained Arguedas, that caused him to weep like his friend in the dialogue above.

He spent his life trying to understand why people he grew up with and loved were brutally treated by the members of his own social class, by his father and relatives who owned so much land and wielded so much power. As a child he had heard the beautiful music and poetry of Quechua *campesinos* and knew them as sensitive, kind people. They were his friends and first teachers and were despised by his own immediate family. Arguedas was caught in a painful dilemma since he felt closer to the oppressed than to his own oppressive class. His escape from this agony was writing, which helped vent some of the anger and self-questioning that so often threatened to overwhelm him.

Arguedas found in Catholicism neither personal solace nor an adequate explanation for the suffering of the poor. To the contrary, he felt the church was one of the principal causes of oppression since it sided with landowners by preaching other-worldly compensation to people who suffered in the here-and-now. He described himself as an agnostic, not because he rejected Christianity as a matter of principle, but because he could not abide what he considered an immoral ecclesiastical institution that lived off human suffering. In the same dialogue from *Deep Rivers* quoted above Arguedas portrays what he considered to be the treason of the church. The passage that follows is one of bitter condemnation and a masterful denunciation of the church's duplicity. Priests who supposedly serve the poor abandon them in need. They leave them disoriented and in even greater pain.

Every year the Franciscan priests go to those haciendas to preach. You should see them, Ernesto! They speak in Quechua, bringing consolation to the Indians and making them sing mournful hymns. The *colonos* crawl around the hacienda chapels on their knees; moaning and groaning, they touch their faces to the ground and weep, day and night. And when the priests leave, you should see them! The Indians follow them. The priests ride off rapidly and the Indians run after them, calling out to them, leaping over fences, bushes and ditches, taking short cuts; shouting, they fall down, only to stumble to their feet again to climb the hills. They come back at night, and go on sobbing in the chapel doorways. My mother used to wear herself out trying to comfort me on such days, and never succeeded.[4]

The *campesinos,* those who represent the other half of Arguedas's person, clearly want the priests to stay. They want to hear of a life-giving God who can console them. And yet the priests only elicit mournful hymns from people who have sung them far too often. Arguedas found it hard to contain his contempt for such priests and the church they represented. But despite his anti-clericalism and agnosticism he never ceased searching for what he called the "God who unites." He constantly sought healing and wholeness that could transcend the pain and fragmentation of his country and inner self.

Gutiérrez and Arguedas met for the first time in the late 1960s. Although brief, their friendship was profound, as the dedication in *A Theology of Liberation* attests. Confronted with the same oppressive reality, both men sought solutions for the seeming hopelessness that surrounded them and found glimmerings of an answer in each other's vision and commitment to the poor. In an article published in 1980 Gutiérrez recounts his first meeting with Arguedas:

I met Arguedas in the last year and a half of his life. José María was in Chimbote preparing his last work and had a chance to read a talk that I had given in Chimbote on liberation theology. That was the reason for the contact we had a few weeks later in Lima. In that first meeting the conversation revolved almost entirely around the meaning of a God who liberates for indigenous Peruvians, for the poor of our country, and for himself. And every time we saw each other during the last year of his life an important theme was that of this God who liberates to whom he refers several times in the work which is considered his last diary [*El zorro de arriba y el zorro de abajo*].[5]

The interview with Gutiérrez is both poignant and revealing. Although people were aware of the friendship between the two men, Gutiérrez waited more than ten years after Arguedas's death to speak about its depth.

It is ironic that Arguedas, an avowed non-believer, would form a friendship with Gutiérrez. At the time the latter was a little known university chaplain giving a series of theological lectures on what would eventually form the basis for *A Theology of Liberation.* Nonetheless, the two men quickly sensed that they had a common interest and quest: to understand the poor and give voice to the voiceless. Their friendship was one of mutual support and commitment. Arguedas saw Gutiérrez as someone who could help him approach and understand the God he perceived among the poor but lacked the words and religious experience to describe. Gutiérrez saw Arguedas as a person who had lived out Peru's agony in his own person and, in the midst of that inner conflict, had found a source of strength in the lives and words of Quechua *campesinos.*

One way to describe the depth of friendship and mutual influence between Gutiérrez and Arguedas is to cite their own words about and to each other. Ten years after Arguedas's death a number of articles appeared about his role in Peruvian literary history. One of the best analyses was written by Gutiérrez himself. In the words that follow he speaks of Arguedas as a key figure in Peru's "impatient struggle to assume form":

> The work of José María Arguedas continues calling us to task. This questioning cannot be responded to by bracketing what he said, that would be artificial and evasive, but only in the midst of this country's tiring struggle for life—which is Peru itself. In truth, José María's voice is heard, ever so paradoxically, in the midst of our national wrangling. The tone of his voice cannot be heard appropriately unless it is accompanied by the unequal chorus of voices—in Quechua and Spanish, of joy and pain, of liberation and oppression, of life and death, which is part of this country. The stridency of those voices in the last ten years is perhaps the real reason why that clamor is more and more part of our national consciousness. In Arguedas there is a coherent, painfully urgent and, for that reason, hope-giving vision of Peru without which his writing is incomprehensible.[6]

According to Gutiérrez, then, Arguedas's genius lies in recognizing the dialectical struggle between rich and poor, *mestizo* and *campesino,* as an inherent quality of Peru itself. The pain of this tension and the cries it produces are part of a larger vision given expression in Quechua and the rough Spanish of the poor. They, and not elite intellectuals, define what it means to be Peruvian. This theme is basic to Gutiérrez's theology and synonymous with what he calls the power of the poor in history.

The relationship between the two men should not be portrayed as one-sided. Arguedas found a source of new ideas and personal support in Gutiérrez. His struggle to find a future-giving God in the midst of so much social and psychological anguish was given new impetus by Gutiérrez's theology, which he read with tremendous excitement. Because it coincided with his own deeply felt intuition that God was somehow present among the poor, it seems to have affirmed him and freed him from what might be called a reactive agnosticism induced by an exploitative institutional church. Ironically, a crusty anti-cleric found a source of hope in the theology of a young priest. This becomes clear in a very personal letter that he wrote to Gutiérrez toward the end of his life.

> Even until the end of his life José María affirmed his faith in the future. If you will permit me, I would like to quote a letter that I received in August of 1969. "Dear Gustavo: I think I have finished the novel, although somewhat abruptly. Your letter arrived at a very opportune moment. I had some very, very rough days. They had begun when we saw each other. Your visit did me a great deal of good. Reading the words you wrote in Chimbote and having had a chance to be with you strengthened *my faith in a future which cannot fail me.* How marvelous that we understand and see each other, together enjoying a light that no one can extinguish."[7]

The novel Arguedas refers to is *El zorro de arriba y el zorro de abajo,* which most critics consider his most powerful and demanding work. In it he portrays his country as a hopeless whirl of irrational oppression and death. *El zorro de arriba,* the fox from above, the indigenous Peruvian from the *sierra* who made up part of Arguedas's own consciousness, cannot come to terms with *el zorro de abajo,* the fox from below, the Spanish-speaking *mestizo* who also formed part of Arguedas's person.

The two foxes are engaged in constant debate. They struggle to understand each other, but the struggle is inconclusive since they distrust and misunderstand each others' words. What makes this novel especially wrenching is that it begins with a number of diary entries in which Arguedas discusses why he intends to commit suicide when the work is completed. The pain and despair of Peruvian society were his own, as is clear from his letter to Gutiérrez. He believed in a future, but not one that he himself would see. Tragically, he decided to end his own life. The fact that this tortured man found a modicum of peace before his death is a profound tribute to Gutiérrez both as a theologian and friend.

Arguedas's death had a profound impact on Peruvians who shared his sensitivity and insights into the lives of the poor. Although clearly due to his personal history and struggle with depression, his suicide was also indicative of the deep distress a person of conscience feels when confronted by exploitation. Arguedas struggled against oppression yet found himself isolated and incapacitated by the complex and often ambiguous phenomena that confronted him. Aware that his society and own person were partially penetrated by pervasive classism and racism responsible for the oppression of millions of Peruvians, he looked for a solution without ever finding one that was truly adequate. In *We Drink from Our Own Wells*, Gutiérrez quotes from Arguedas's last novel, where he discusses his struggle with death, his own and that of the poor:

> I have struggled against death, or at least I believe I have struggled against death, very straightforwardly, by writing this broken and querulous account. My allies were few and unreliable; the allies of death won out. They are strong and were looked upon with favor by my own flesh. This account with its roughness reflects that unequal fight.[8]

Arguedas often characterized that inner and social struggle as a fight against the false and oppressive values of *mestizos* and the ideological structures they use to maintain their dominance. He describes the way lawyers, politicians, police, and the clergy conspire to hold together an unjust and malignant social order. He also portrays how their victims both acquiesce and resist their power. Dominated by a culture and socio-economic system not of their own making, the *campesinos* and urban workers of Arguedas's novels both internalize their oppression and fight it. The resistance they offer flows from their sense of cultural uniqueness. They possess a distinct *mito*, or vision of reality, whose roots are Andean. Although repressed, the culture of the *campesinos* still survives and keeps alive an alternate vision of society. It is their source of hope and key to survival.

Despite the misery around him, Arguedas managed to perceive the outline of a utopian vision, albeit imperfectly, among those who formed "the fellowship of the wretched."[9] This juxtaposition of good and evil in society is what gives his works such poignancy and realism. His novels are filled with "anonymous heroes"[10] from the most exploited contexts who struggle against the ideology of their dominators. Despite their broken Spanish and seeming ignorance, the oppressed skirmish with the established powers. Although often vanquished, they occasionally win small victories. Gutiérrez knows first hand that the world Arguedas describes is not a literary invention. The struggles and people in his novels have real counterparts in the day-to-day world. Gutiérrez continually sees them in the *comunidades de base* and movements for liberation that he has helped form and continues to participate in, as the following passage makes clear:

> In search of this utopia, an entire people — with all its traditional values and the wealth of its recent experience — has taken to the path of building a world in which persons are more important than things and in which all can live with dignity, a society that respects

human freedom when it is in the service of a genuine common good, and exercises no kind of coercion, from whatever source.[11]

This utopian vision springs from the belief of ordinary people in a "God who rejoins" — a phrase Arguedas used frequently and Gutiérrez has incorporated as a key concept in his theology. Unlike the divinity of Spanish Catholicism who is distant and severe, the God who rejoins nourishes and makes whole. Much like the *Pachamama,* or Earth Mother, *campesinos* have reverenced for centuries, Arguedas's God sustains the community of the oppressed with the gifts of nature and a collective belief in life. This is the God who makes whole and "rejoins the 'popular' struggles for liberation and the hope of the exploited."[12]

We must bear in mind that the poor are not romanticized by either Arguedas or Gutiérrez. They accept them for who they are, people whose lives are "partially penetrated" by the violence that surrounds them. Arguedas's novels are studies in the effects of deprivation. The behavior of the oppressed can be as mean as their oppressors'. Arguedas was adept at describing the fatalism and self-destructive behavior so characteristic of the Andes and Peruvian coast. Gutiérrez is equally realistic:

> Contrary to what a certain romantic notion would hold, the world of the poor is not made up simply of victims, of solidarity and the struggle for human rights. The universe of the poor is inhabited by flesh-and-blood human beings, pervaded with the forces of life and death, of grace and sin. In that world we find indifference to others, individualism, abandoned children, people abusing people, pettiness, hearts closed to the action of the Lord. Insofar as the poor are part of human history, they are not free of the motivations found in the two cities of which St. Augustine spoke: love of God and love of self.[13]

Yet, drawing from Arguedas's writings, Gutiérrez insists that liberation has to take place in the "universe of the poor" despite its defects. "Radical liberation" requires that the poor come to terms with their own participation in the oppressive structures that surround them. The "anonymous heroes" of Arguedas's novels and Gutiérrez's *comunidades de base* are people whose vision flows out of self-knowledge and realism. They alone can change society.

The relationship between Arguedas and Gutiérrez, like any deep friendship, cannot be adequately communicated in a few paragraphs. Furthermore, despite Arguedas's death, we might say that their friendship still lives and grows in Gutiérrez's continuing quest to make liberation a reality. Yet certain of their shared ideas deserve reiteration. For both men the situation of oppression they describe requires a fundamental choice. Either one sides with the oppressor or the oppressed. Despite the "partial penetration" of the poor and their faults, either one is for or against them. This choice determines one's political options. To choose the poor is to opt for a different world and actively help to create it. Secondly, an option for the poor is an option for a different God. Gutiérrez insists on this point: "I believe José María was right. . . . The God of the oppressors, of those who pillage and kill people, is not the God of the poor, not the same God at all."[14] Arguedas and Gutiérrez both came to realize that the God of the dominator is merely a distorted image of the oppressor's own desire for domination. "The God of the poor" is a God made present in their struggle for liberation. Arguedas's gift to Gutiérrez was a deep and poetic appreciation of the poor. He provided him with a way of incorporating their language and experience into his theology. Gutiérrez's gift was a vision of a liberating God Arguedas perhaps now sees more clearly.

José Carlos Mariátegui

The numerous references to José Carlos Mariátegui in Gutiérrez's writings are apt to slip by readers unfamiliar with Latin American political thought. Mariátegui, however, was one of Peru's foremost social theorists. Although he died more than sixty years ago, he continues to influence the political imaginations of his compatriots. His ideas are part of everyday political language in Peru. An unpretentious person gifted with an acute intellect and formidable powers of expression, he was one of the first Peruvians to synthesize Marxist social theory and originally apply its insights to his own country. In the 1920s when most Marxists explained nearly everything in terms of deterministic economic theory, he realized that Peru's greatest affliction was racism and classism working in tandem. He saw beyond the merely economic to the human. Mariátegui had the genius and courage to point to the theoretical and elitist principles that influenced political leaders, both of the left and of the right. His description of Peru is disarmingly blunt:

> It is a country in which Indians and foreign conquerors live side by side but do not mingle with or even understand one another. . . . The feelings and interests of four-fifths of the population play almost no role in the formation of the national identity and institutions.[15]

Although most of his writings were composed in the twenties, including his masterpiece, *Seven Interpretive Essays on Peruvian Reality,* they continue to be relevant. Social classes in Peru still do not mingle nor understand each other and the interests of four-fifths of the population are still ignored. Perhaps one small but hopeful difference between then and now is that the poor are more aware of the fact.

For many Peruvians Mariátegui remains a source of national pride. He was the first person to examine the inner workings of Peruvian history from the viewpoint of the oppressed. Gutiérrez sums up his perception of Mariátegui and evaluates his importance as follows:

> Mariátegui is especially significant for Peruvian culture. It is he who, for the first time, tries to think out the Peruvian historical process and the Peruvian reality of his time with new and distinct categories which have had an enormous impact on the way we understand our society. I have had the opportunity to work through Mariátegui for academic reasons. For several years in the University I taught a course dedicated entirely to Mariátegui's ideas. . . . In my opinion he combines many qualities. He is significant because his action and thought arise from his experience of the popular classes.[16]

At a time when a European education and bourgeois bearing were considered indispensable for both political leaders and intellectuals, Mariátegui had the audacity to point to the wisdom and integrity of the poor as foundational elements for a new order. Long before the concept was used, he recognized that the "organic intelligence" of ordinary people was crucial for reshaping his country's future. Obviously, there is a contiguous line of thought which links together his style of social analysis, Arguedas's novels, and Gutiérrez's theology. Each has incorporated the viewpoint of the poor as a key methodological principle, be it in journalism, literature, or theology.

Mariátegui's sensitivity to the oppressed is explained by the circumstances of his early life. Born in the southern city of Tacna in 1895 to a poor *mestizo* family, he learned early lessons in survival. Abandoned by his father, he was forced to leave primary school after a few grades and look for work. Despite persistent problems with tuberculosis that would cost him his life in 1930, Mariátegui was apprenticed to a printer. Studying on his own he learned the rudiments of journalism and managed to support his mother and family by writing short articles. In his teens he migrated to Lima where he found work as a copy boy for one of the principal papers. Despite his lack of formal education, he managed to move up in the world of journalism and eventually became a popular columnist. Yet his allegiance to the poor was not diminished by success. He never forgot his own early struggles nor the social class from which he came.

As a reporter on the Lima scene, Mariátegui became progressively more critical of existing social structures, and his point of view was bluntly expressed in his daily columns and frequent essays. His condemnation of the landed families that controlled Peru at the time eventually earned him several years of exile in Europe where, with his exposure to Marxism, his understanding of capitalism became more focused and critical. He returned to Lima for the last few years of his life with a sophisticated knowledge of Marxism and dedicated himself to making socialism a working proposition in Peru. Through his writings and efforts at political organizing he established the basis for the Peruvian Communist Party.

An interesting facet of Mariátegui's personal development is that before he turned to Marxism he was a fervent Catholic. In his late teens he made a retreat with the Carmelites, which had an impact on the course of his adult life. Reading the gospels he became conscious of the need for what he called "faith," a belief in people's potential to create a new, more just social order. He understood the message of Jesus as both a call to interior conversion and social action incumbent on all, but particularly the poor. Reflecting on his own upbringing in poverty and the deep religious faith of his mother, Mariátegui realized that the familial Catholicism he was exposed to as a boy was a powerful force of sustenance that could transform personal behavior and reshape society. Once faith was purified of excessively individualistic pietism it could serve as a powerful, future-oriented symbol.

As Mariátegui became more politically sensitive in his twenties he left the institutional church, which, in his opinion, had betrayed the gospel because of its ties to the oligarchy and preoccupation with power. Nonetheless, he always maintained a deep respect for the "popular religiosity" and culture of Peruvians to which he dedicated several provocative essays. To the consternation of certain hard-line Marxists, he perceived and affirmed something positive and helpful in the faith of the poor. He refused to glibly dismiss their religiosity as an expression of alienation.

Mariátegui's ability to reconcile certain aspects of Christianity and popular belief with Marxism set a unique precedent that has allowed elements of the Peruvian popular movement to take a deeper, more culturally sensitive approach to religious practices. In many ways, Mariátegui anticipated what we now call Christian-Marxist dialogue by nearly forty years. Because of his influence the unfortunate breach between the left and religious believers that has characterized so much European history in the last two centuries has been less present in Peru, although not entirely absent. As Jeffrey Klaiber points out, the mixture of Marxism and Christianity in Mariátegui's writings is such that it is sometimes hard to decide where his primary loyalties lay:

> Was Mariátegui a Christian in search of a new faith, viz., Marxism, or was he, in fact, a Marxist convinced that he should return to the Christianity of his youth?[17]

The question, however, is somewhat academic as Mariátegui felt no contradiction between a critically appropriated faith and a commitment to radical political change. He realized that what was most profound and even most revolutionary in Peruvian culture was its religio-poetic depth and felt that it was compatible with Marxism as he understood it. As Klaiber notes:

> Mariátegui perceived religion as a dynamic element in people which

inspired them to act and sustained their actions. . . . In periods of social transition, religion could serve as an oppositional force to the dominant culture, offering people a vision of a new order as an alternative to the present state of affairs. In order to give this concept of religion a broader sense, Mariátegui preferred to include religion within the concept of "myth."[18]

In Mariátegui's opinion the beliefs of ordinary *campesinos,* steeped as they are in Andean traditions that view the earth and life as a collective trust of God, have an inherently socialistic character. They are based on a collective self-identity and communal religious experience distinct from the individualistic Catholicism of the *mestizo.* The religious "myth" of the *campesinos* serves as a force that unites "spirit and matter"[19] for ordinary people instead of separating them. As the passage below makes clear, Mariátegui insisted that Marxists stop glibly categorizing the religion of the oppressed as mere superstition and examine its deeper meaning:

> We have already definitely left behind the days of anti-clerical prejudice when the "free-thinking" critic happily discarded all dogmas and churches in favor of the dogma and church of the atheist's free-thinking orthodoxy. The concept of religion has become broader and deeper, going far beyond a church and a sacrament. It now finds in religion's institutions and sentiments a significance very different from that which was attributed to it by those fervent radicals who identified religion with "obscurantism."[20]

The tension between faith and politics consequently disappears in Mariátegui's writings, much as it does in those of Gutiérrez. The dividing line is not between Christians and Marxists, but between those who support the ideology of the status quo and those who struggle for a new social order.

Gutiérrez constantly acknowledges his debt to Mariátegui and it is quite easy to see the correlation between their respective terms and concepts. The "myth" that unites "spirit and matter" is closely allied with what Gutiérrez call the "utopic vision" of the poor, which links faith and political action:

> Like others, I am interested in what Christianity means for the life, struggles, and culture of the Peruvian people or, to say it in Mariátegui's terms, in the role of the religious factor in the historical process of the people. I am not interested in it as an expression of "Catholic thought" or as a social concern like certain intellectuals are who live in ivory towers. I refer to something much more profound, to something which can only come from the oppressed working class: to how Christianity enters into the process of popular liberation, in the construction of a nation. There is a lot here to explore, a new field of creativity which resides in the people who are both exploited and in

possession of a deep Christian faith which fights for liberation. It is a question of a path which will allow us to rediscover the liberating God whom Josá María Arguedas called "The God Who Rejoins."[21]

Both Mariátegui's and Gutiérrez's perception of popular religion and culture as the seedbed for social change is more than a hypothesis. As we saw previously, the Las Casas team has demonstrated a clear, albeit complex, connection between the faith of the poor and their political action, which they continue to explore.

The more "flexible" Marxism of Mariátegui with its openness to popular culture and religion can be explained by the people who mediated his exposure to Marx's ideas during his years of exile in France and Italy. As Klaiber notes, he studied Marxism with "thinkers like Sorel, Croce and Labriola"[22] who rejected the rigid Marxism of their day. Although they accepted the validity of certain of Marx's theories, they refused to canonize them as immutable truths. Wary of left-wing dogmatism and elitism, they advocated participatory socialism as the most effective solution for Italian society. Because of their influence Mariátegui avoided the danger of turning Marxism into a fetish. In his own words, it was not

... a corpus of principles with rigid, pre-determined outcomes, equally applicable for all historical contexts and social arrangements but rather a *method of interpretation* in each country ... [which] functions and acts on the general context, on the social medium, without disregarding any of its characteristics.[23]

Mariátegui insisted that Marxism had to be "contextualized" in order to respond to the socio-political history and culture of Peru. He considered Marxism a "method for the historical interpretation of society, not a philosophy of history"[24] that had to be blindly followed. Mariátegui was all too aware that a people's hope of liberation, like the liberation of God, varies with age, country, and climate. He was quite cognizant of the "philosophical astigmatism"[25] of certain Marxists who, in his opinion, represented a real danger to the interests of ordinary Peruvians.

Gutiérrez's understanding of socialism clearly owes a great deal to Mariátegui. He spells this out in *A Theology of Liberation:*

For Mariátegui as for many today in Latin America, historical materialism is above all "a method for the historical interpretation of society." All his work, thought, and action — although not exempt from understandable limitations — was characterized by these concerns. His socialism was creative because it was fashioned in loyalty. He was loyal to his sources, that is, to the central intuitions of Marx, yet was beyond all dogmatism; he was simultaneously loyal to a unique historical reality.[26]

The loyalty and lack of dogmatism in Mariátegui's vision are what continue to make his insights applicable today. As Gutiérrez and others recognize, accurate political assessment and action are aided by an open political mind unencumbered by party dogmas. Mariátegui knew Marx's works well enough not to absolutize them. The same is true of Gutiérrez.

Gutiérrez draws several lessons from Mariátegui that directly influence his understanding of the socio-theological task of liberation. Perhaps the most obvious is that one's political or theological posture cannot be "unqualifiedly transposed to other situations."[27] Context and history are crucial considerations that influence the applicability of any viewpoint. The first factor to be considered is the social and historical reality of a people. As Mariátegui insisted, it is the starting point for social change. Theory conforms to reality and not the opposite.

Furthermore, Gutiérrez, much like Mariátegui, insists that "only a sufficiently broad, rich, and intense revolutionary praxis, with the participation of people of different viewpoints, can create the condition for fruitful theory."[28] In other words, only a liberation movement capable of incorporating the insights of urban workers as well as indigenous *campesinos* can really effect social change and avoid the ever-present danger of left-wing sectarianism. Unfortunately, the Peruvian left has a tragic history of hair-splitting debate and internecine bloodletting about the "correctness" and applicability of imported political theories. Gutiérrez suggests that the most productive course of action is to leave this negative legacy behind and create a truly indigenous socialism.

> One of the great dangers which threatens the building of socialism in Latin America — pressed as it is by immediate concerns — is the lack of its own solid theory. And this theory must be Latin American, not to satisfy a desire for originality, but for the sake of elementary historical realism.[29]

For Gutiérrez liberation and socialism must correspond to the experience and aspirations of ordinary people. The only "solid theory" is the one that they construct. Ultimately, it is the only theory that makes sense and has any political future.

Mariátegui, like Arguedas, has provided Gutiérrez with a special Peruvian focal point with which to view his own country. In fact, we cannot understand his theology adequately without reference to the role of these two people in its development. They have shaped his self-perception as a Christian and political values more than anyone else. Arguedas provided Gutiérrez with many of the words he uses to express his compassion for and commitment to the poor. Mariátegui's writings have helped him develop an awareness of the latent political power of ordinary Peruvians whose right it is to shape their country in accord with their needs and vision.

Gutiérrez's critics sometimes accuse him of being a misguided intellectual removed from the concerns of ordinary people. If this were the case he never would have been a friend of Arguedas nor live in Rimac. Gutiérrez is indeed an intellectual, but his knowledge flows from and is at the service of his own people. Likewise, some claim that Gutiérrez, along with other liberation theologians, approach Marxism naïvely.[30] But someone as versed in the contextualized socialism of Mariátegui would not commit such a blunder. Gutiérrez has spent a great deal of time studying Marxist thought, but he has done so critically as Mariátegui insisted. This should be kept in mind as we enter the realm of Marxist socio-political theory in the chapter that follows.

NOTES

1. José María Arguedas, *Deep Rivers*, trans. Frances Horning Barraclough (Austin: University of Texas, 1978), p. vii.
2. This phrase, which is a key concept in Arguedas's novels, surfaces constantly in almost all of Gutiérrez's writings, particularly *We Drink from Our Own Wells* and *On Job.*
3. *Deep Rivers*, p. 145.
4. Ibid., pp. 145–146.
5. Luis Peirano, Entrevista con Gustavo Gutiérrez, *Quehacer* (March 1980): p. 115.
6. Gustavo Gutiérrez, *Entre las calandrias* (Lima: Centro de Estudios y Publicaciones, 1982), pp. 242–243.
7. Ibid., pp. 252–253, note 19.
8. Gutiérrez, *We Drink from Our Own Wells: The Spiritual Journey of a People* (Maryknoll, N.Y.: Orbis Books, and Melbourne: Dove Communications, 1984), p. 152.
9. Ibid., p. 21.
10. Ibid.
11. Ibid., p. 27.
12. Gutiérrez and Shaull, *Liberation and Change,* ed. Ronald H. Stone (Atlanta: John Knox, 1977), p. 93.
13. Gutiérrez, *We Drink from Our Own Wells*, p. 125.
14. Peirano, p. 115.
15. José Carlos Mariátegui, *Seven Interpretive Essays on Peruvian Reality*, trans. Marjory Urquidi (Austin: University of Texas Press, 1971), p. 78.
16. As quoted in Peirano, p. 117.
17. Jeffrey Klaiber, *Religión y revolución en el Perú 1824–1976*, (Lima: Universidad del Pácifico, 1980), p. 120.
18. Ibid., p. 130.
19. Ibid., p. 137.
20. Mariátegui, p. 124.
21. Peirano, p. 115.
22. Klaiber, p. 129.
23. As quoted in Miguel Manzanera, *Teología y salvación en la obra de Gustavo Gutiérrez* (Bilbao: University of Deusto, 1978), p. 131. Manzanera is a Spanish Jesuit who works in Bolivia. The above text is from his doctoral dissertation which focuses on Gutiérrez's theological method.
24. Ibid.
25. Mariátegui, *Seven Interpretive Essays*, p. 75, note 15.

26. Gutiérrez, *A Theology of Liberation*, p. 90.
27. Ibid., p. 284, note 49.
28. Ibid., p. 90.
29. Ibid., pp. 90–91.
30. This accusation is made in the documents issued by the Congregation for the Doctrine of the Faith on liberation theology. On page 199, paragraph 6, of the first instruction it is stated that liberation theologians cannot separate the positive and negative aspects of Marxism and consequently accept the totality of the Marxist tradition. The document claims that this explains "why it is not uncommon for the ideological aspect to be predominant among the things which the 'theologians of liberation' borrow from Marxist authors." Such an accusation cannot be reconciled with Gutiérrez's writings. See "Instruction on Certain Aspects of the 'Theology of Liberation' from the Congregation for the Doctrine of the Faith," *Origins* 14 (September 13, 1984): pp. 1, 195–204, and also "Instruction on Christian Freedom and Liberation by the Congregation for the Doctrine of the Faith," *Origins* 15 (April 17, 1986): pp. 713, 715–728.

Chapter 4

Marxism, Social Science, and Class Struggle

In this chapter we shall explore some extremely delicate and frequently misunderstood topics: how Gutiérrez understands Marxism, the role of the social sciences in his theology, and the relationship between class struggle and liberation. Unfortunately these questions have been blown entirely out of proportion by the two documents on liberation theology issued by the Congregation for the Doctrine of the Faith and the yellow journalism of the conservative political establishment. If only to dispel false notions borne of poor analysis and fear, it is crucial that we grapple with Gutiérrez's approach to these complex issues.

We shall first examine how Gutiérrez responds to four key Marxist thinkers — Marx himself, Althusser, Gramsci, and Bloch. All these authors are cited by Gutiérrez, and analyzing how he approaches them will help us appreciate just how selective his use of the Marxist tradition actually is. If nothing else, I hope our discussion will put to rest the notion that Gutiérrez is a Marxist in disguise. As he notes in *The Power of the Poor in History,* an encounter with the social sciences and Marxist analysis[1] is inevitable for Latin American theologians. But familiarity with Marxism does not make him a Marxist nor is such knowledge necessarily bad. Next we shall analyze Gutiérrez's approach to the social sciences and his understanding of class struggle. Again, these are "hot" topics. The first statement on liberation theology issued by Rome states that certain theologians, and one can only presume that Gutiérrez is among them, are naïve about the limitations of social analysis, particularly the Marxist variety. They are also supposedly blithe about the dangers of class struggle as a theme in Christian theology. Fortunately, Gutiérrez has responded directly and clearly to those who question the use of such topics in his writings. In 1984 he wrote an important article in the Peruvian journal *Páginas,*[2] which explains his understanding of the social sciences and the relationship between class struggle and the liberation of the poor.

Gutiérrez's Theology and the Marxist Tradition:
Similarities and Differences

Marx

The ideas of Karl Marx are quite familiar to Gustavo Gutiérrez and figure prominently in his earlier writings such as *A Theology of Liberation*. During his studies in Belgium and France Gutiérrez developed a sophisticated knowledge of Marx's writings and the the Marxist tradition in general. He was also exposed to the Christian-Marxist dialogue taking place in Europe during the 1960s. Through the writings of theologians such as Guilio Girardi he began to appreciate the utility of Marx's ideas in interpreting the dynamics of Western capitalistic society and the challenge they present to the contemporary Christian.

Gutiérrez focused primarily on Marx the historian, the successor and synthesizer of Hegel, rather than on the political economist and author of *Capital*. This point may seem tangential, but is nonetheless important. The ideas of Marx that Gutiérrez employs in his theology are those that explain the human, historical effects of capitalism. Marx's studies of phenomena such as the accumulation of surplus labor and class stratification in industrial society are useful for understanding the causes of poverty and oppression in Third World countries such as Peru. But accepting the validity of certain of Marx's ideas does not mean that Gutiérrez accepts the latter's overall vision. He rejects the materialism and economic determinism characteristic of Marx as antithetical to real, integral liberation and human freedom.

Drawing from the studies of the French historian Lucien Goldmann, Gutiérrez sees Marx's writings as an inevitable reaction to socio-economic naïvete of the first phase of the Enlightenment. As set forth in the philosophy of Kant and Hegel, the Enlightenment was a time of unbridled promise later betrayed by "its own inner contradictions."[3] The call to create a society "free of all alienation and servitude"[4] was subverted by the oppression of laissez-faire capitalism and the distorted definition of society and human life that stood behind it. Marx's genius lay in his ability to assess the shortcomings of the Enlightenment, while reshaping its emancipatory message into a more realistic, historically oriented vision of society.

For Gutiérrez the promise of the Enlightenment is most visible in Hegel's understanding of history, which Marx helped disseminate and concretize. By demonstrating the centrality of history and the role of human agents in its evolution, Hegel and Marx precipitated an epistemological revolution that turned philosophy and traditional definitions of society upside down.

> From a cosmological vision, man moves to an anthropological vision, due especially to scientific developments. Man perceives himself as a creative subject. Moreover, man becomes aware ... that he is an agent

of history, responsible for his own destiny. His mind discovers not only
the laws of nature, but also penetrates those of society, history, and
psychology.[5]

At its deepest level history is a "genesis of conscience" in which people
are called to become "creative subjects" capable of understanding the world
and their responsibility in shaping it. History is a "gradual conquest of lib-
erty" in which human beings "generate themselves dialectically"[6] through
their efforts to attain freedom.

Marx realized, however, that Hegel's moving but abstract vision of freedom and self-determination was far removed from the squalor and oppression produced by nineteenth-century capitalism. Hegel had a magnificent,
sweeping sense of history, but little knowledge of the misery and hopelessness most German laborers experienced as their daily fare. According to
the tenets of Hegel's philosophy the purpose of labor was to allow people
to construct society in a free and just manner. Yet the labor power of
the ordinary worker had been turned into a commodity bought and sold
by the bourgeoisie. European workers were hardly able to keep body and
soul together, much less ruminate on the meaning of history. It was Marx
who realized that if Hegel's call for historical self-determination was to
have any impact it had to be reshaped and brought down to earth. It
had to be converted into a vision somehow capable of overcoming the dehumanizing ruthlessness of capitalism. This required understanding the
relationship among a society's beliefs and values, economic activity, and
historical shape. And that ambitious project engaged Marx for most of his
life.

Analyzing his social context Marx realized that one of the principal
pillars of the capitalist belief system was the dogma of individualism. The
role model for the successful, fulfilled human being was the economically
independent, discrete individual who functioned in the market place of free
exchange. Paraphrasing Marx's words, Gutiérrez summarizes the basic
tenets of bourgeois individualism as follows:

> Individualism is the most important aspect of bourgeois ideology. It
> is expressed, for the modern mentality, in the conception of the indi-
> vidual as an absolute beginning, an autonomous center of decisions.
> Individual initiative and interest are the starting point and motor of
> economic activity.[7]

A person's worth is accordingly measured by his or her individualism,
that is, the amount of autonomy that can be purchased through private
property and the acquisition of wealth. In actual practice human dignity
is gauged in capitalist society by material possessions and social power,
rather than by inner spirit and a sense of collective responsibility.

Gutiérrez realizes that Marx's exposé of the negative role of individualism points to real theological issues. The excessive individualism charac-

teristic of capitalism effectively negates the biblical mandate of solidarity between brothers and sisters. It pits one person against another in a never-ending, Darwinian struggle for dominance that is hardly reconcilable with the message of the gospel. Inadvertently, then, Marx helps explain a palpable form of sinfulness in contemporary society.

Marx realized that personal freedom and self-determination were illusions in societies characterized by competition among individuals and social classes. In his opinion such values functioned "ideologically," that is, they distorted and covered over the real nature of society. The bourgeoisie of his time was enthralled by an endless quest for capital accumulation and the social power it provided. And the working class whose labor the bourgeoisie "appropriated" was often too numb and exploited to think of anything except sheer survival.

Again, in words that closely resemble those of Marx, Gutiérrez points out that the acquisition of wealth was and continues to be the guiding value of capitalist society, not freedom or self-determination.

> The demands for individual freedom and social equality are thus related to the new economic forms. Similarly, the right to private property is fundamental for bourgeois society, for above all, this right concerns the matter of ownership of the means of production. "The freedom of industry," wrote G. de Ruggiero, "is the daughter of modern individualism; even more it is its favorite daughter." Social equality also has a clear economic reference: persons are equal in the moment of buying and selling. Furthermore, the formal equality is a condition of mercantile activity.[8]

The belief that equality exists "in the moment of buying and selling," however, contradicts the dynamics of capital accumulation. Those who own the means of production enjoy an "equality" others cannot obtain in a class stratified society. Yet we are dealing with one of the most sacred and accepted tenets of capitalism. In Marx's terms, we are confronted with a prime example of ideology, a self-contradictory but pervasive version of reality propagated and maintained by those with socio-economic power.

Both in Marx's day and now the negative effects of capitalism are covered over by appealing to abstract, ideological definitions of human nature. As Gutiérrez points out, capitalism claims to reflect who we are — competitive beasts who stalk a jungle known as the free market. Economic competition is accordingly a "logical" and inevitable facet of human behavior.

> The different individual interests find a regulation in the market: the law of supply and demand. This law makes the free play of individual interests coincide with the general interest. This coincidence thus results in a natural order. It is not something forced by an authority

which arbitrarily imposes and decides what is to be done. Rather, it occurs naturally. This is the origin of the idea that capitalism is the economic regime natural to the human person.[9]

Gutiérrez knows from experience, however, that "the free play of individual interests" has nothing to do "with the general interest" of society. He need only describe the dehumanization of Lima's *pueblos jovenes* to refute this cherished piece of capitalist belief that Marx criticized long ago. Furthermore, the daily lot of the poor is neither logical nor natural. It is, rather, the result of a sinful social situation created and sustained by the self-interest of a specific class.

Another of Marx's insights Gutiérrez finds useful is his analysis of the way labor power is turned into a source of alienation and social marginalization by the inner logic of capitalism. Because the ultimate point of reference in capitalism is wealth, those who have little or none are classified as lesser beings whose lives and labor can be utilized as those in power deem best. Since labor is seen as a commodity rather than an expression of human creativity, it can be used with no reference to its human source. Intent on appropriating the labor of the working class, those who control the means of production create a "reserve industrial pool" of "marginalized people"[10] whose energy is exploited to reproduce the status quo. Consequently what is deepest and most sacred in human nature, namely, our power to work and create, is torn away from the poor. Their labor ends up being a source of alienation rather than an affirmation of their humanity. In Gutiérrez's terms the poor become "non-persons."

Marx's genius was to point out that exploitation and class stratification are inevitable by-products of capitalism. But Marx was not content with mere analysis. He studied capitalism's negative effects in order to find a way of overcoming them. Gutiérrez comments in *A Theology of Liberation:*

> In a famous text Marx points out very precisely his contribution to the class struggle: not the discovery of its existence, but rather the analysis of its causes and an indication of the path to a classless society.... The class struggle is inherent in classist organization of society. The objective which Marx proposes is to abolish that which gives origin to the very existence of social classes. But the causes of the class struggle cannot be overcome without first becoming aware of the struggle and its demands in the process of building a new society.[11]

Gutiérrez draws an important lesson from Marx's observations, namely, that the negative effects of capitalism will not be overcome until the poor understand the real causes of their oppression. They must perceive themselves as agents of history who have the right to shape society according to their own best interests.

Gutiérrez considers Marx's insights something of a "Copernican revolution" that altered the way we view history, society, and the social role of Christians. As he puts it: "History — which according to Marx indissolubly includes nature and society — is seen as the object of change and transformation as well as an agent of self-transformation."[12] Marx challenges us to come to terms with history and society as objective phenomena that are neither sheer material facts outside our control nor mere mental constructs. They are, rather, the concrete results of human endeavor for which we ourselves are responsible. Gutiérrez accordingly believes that people committed to social change, particularly Christians, must learn a crucial lesson from Marx. They must see and appreciate the interplay between the material nature of history and society and the human actors who give them shape.

> Marx situated himself equidistant between the old materialism and idealism; more precisely, he presented his position as the dialectical transcendence of both. Of the first he retained the affirmation of the objectivity of the external world; of the second he kept man's transforming capacity.[13]

Once we are aware of the complex interplay between these two characteristics of history, we achieve a more "scientific" awareness of the world around us. The challenge is to realize that we are, as it were, history, and that history is directly bound up with our material existence. In many ways history is an expression of our physical life. At the same time, however, it is metaphysical to the extent that it transcends each of us as individuals. As Gutiérrez sees it, such a perspective will help "theology to perceive what its efforts at understanding the faith receive from the historical praxis of man in history as well as what its own reflection might mean for the transformation of the world."[14] Marx's insights thus challenge Christian self-understanding and praxis. They require that we assume a critical and responsible role in the making of history in the material, social world.

Gutiérrez, quoting Sartre, feels that "Marxism, as the formal framework of all contemporary philosophical thought, cannot be superseded."[15] Marx set in motion a tradition of scientific social analysis that has helped "man take one more step on the road of critical thinking. It made him more aware of the socio-economic determinants of his ideological creations and therefore freer and more lucid in relation to them."[16] Marx opened the way for a more realistic assessment of society and history — an indispensable component for liberative praxis. But the quest for a truly critical, scientific approach to history and society is a process still in motion. Marx's ideas are not the last word, nor can they be. Despite his undeniable genius and commitment to social change, Marx was blinded to its deeper nature by his myopic materialism. Confined by his own rigidly "scientific" methodology, he failed to understand that the struggle for liberation foreshadows something far greater, namely, full humanity that will be realized in the reign of God. Aware of this, Gutiérrez parts company with Marx, although respectful of his contributions.

Althusser

If Marx's writings were coterminous with Marxism it would be easier to analyze their relationship to Gutiérrez's theology. But such is not the case. To complicate matters even more, Marx's own thoughts are often convoluted and inconsistent in areas of key importance. Even his understanding of ideology shifts from text to text. Not surprisingly, there is constant and sometimes acrimonious debate as to what Marx meant by a given word or concept. Students of Marx's thought inevitably interpret his writings in terms of their own social context and intellectual background. As a cursory glance at Marxist literature quickly proves, the number of interpretations is prodigious and varied.

For weal or woe one of the foremost interpreters of Marx in the second half of this century has been Louis Althusser, who served for many years as the chief theoretician of the French Communist Party. His various studies of Marx, especially *Reading Capital* and *Lenin and Philosophy* have had a profound impact on contemporary left-wing thought. When Gutiérrez was studying in France during the 1960s, Althusser was the principal proponent of a hard-line variety of Marxism. Certain of Gutiérrez's Latin American compatriots quickly became enamored of Althusser's thinking and imported it to their own continent. As we shall shortly see, Gutiérrez is no devotee of Althusserian Marxism, but he has nonetheless grappled with its central premises since it has been an influential current of thought in Latin America.[17]

In Gutiérrez's own words, Althusser attempted to develop a " 'science of history' which tries to free itself from all ideological elements," [18] thus clarifying the real meaning of Marx's ideas. Whether he succeeded, however, is a highly disputed point.[19] A fundamental concept in Althusser's writings is that of "science." He insists that the only accurate and politically effective interpretation of Marx is one that is "scientific." By this he means a reading which has been purged of any trace of idealism or subjectivity, which, in his opinion, are the two vices that most threaten the purity and efficacy of Marxism as a political philosophy and social movement.

In effect, Althusser set out to outdo Marx to the extent that he accused the master himself of unwitting idealism, particularly in his early writings when he was supposedly under Hegel's sway. According to Althusser the late Marx, that is, the hard-nosed economist and author of *Capital,* is the person whose ideas are most cogent and credible. He asserts that in *Capital* Marx set out a "real science" of economics and political philosophy as opposed to his earlier works where idealistic Hegelianism is still too much in evidence. In *Reading Capital*, Althusser provides an exegetical method for getting at the so-called scientific core of Marx's thought.

Judging the validity of Althusser's viewpoint is a labor best left to those skilled in the nuances of Marxist hermeneutics. Our task is more limited. We want to examine how Gutiérrez reacts to his "scientific" interpretation of Marx as a theologian and Third World Christian. As one might surmise, Althusser and his followers have been less than sympathetic to Christianity, which, in their opinion, is unadulterated idealism. Their insistence on an exclusively "scientific," materialist reading of Marx has tended to sustain and sometimes accentuate the gap between the left and Christians committed to radical social change.[20] Given the challenge to Christians presented by Althusser, Gutiérrez has spent a great deal of time assessing his interpretation of Marxism and rejection of Christianity. One of Althusser's principal premises is that the concept of subjectivity, as it is understood in capitalist society, is inherently ideological. He maintains that *the* source and mainstay of capitalism as a socio-economic system is the mistaken belief that we are distinct, autonomous subjects. In his own words, "the category of the subject is constitutive of all ideology."[21] Although Marx was aware that the concept of individuality was crucial to the capitalist ethos, according to Althusser he failed to realize how important this notion was for its maintenance. On the basis of an erroneous understanding of self we compete with each other as discrete sources of capital. Rather than seeing ourselves as part of an organic unity, we act as if we were separate entities, thus living out the ethos of capitalism in our own persons.

The capitalist system reinforces this false notion of self by means of what he calls "ideological apparatuses," or social institutions that tell us in multiple ways that we are distinct individuals and are obligated to act as such.[22] Victims of an exaggerated sense of self, we unwittingly give our lives and labor to a social system that feeds off social fragmentation and the domination of one class by another. In Althusser's opinion one of the primary "ideological apparatuses" in Western society has been the church. By propagating belief in an individual soul and a God who relates to each of us as a unique person, Christianity has been a mainstay of capitalism. We are conditioned by moral training to believe that wealth and power are the result of personal merit and hard work. But the church is only inculcating a false sense of self that "euphemizes" the competitive, classist assumptions of the society we live in. It provides us with what Althusser calls "Beautiful Lies" that blind us to the "real conditions of existence."[23]

Entranced by an exaggerated sense of individuality and convinced that each of us is an autonomous moral and economic agent, we view poverty as personal failure rather than an inherent by-product of the way our society is put together. To the extent that "I" am successful "I" prove that capitalism really is the most effective and satisfactory social system. "My" wealth assuages "my" conscience. The fact that there are poor people is because "they" are either lazy or immoral. According to Althusser, breaking out of this epistemological bind is nearly impossible since we are bombarded with ideological messages from church, school, and mass media. Those few individuals who challenge the assumptions of the status quo are usually branded as dangerous deviants to be shunned and, if necessary, eliminated.

Gutiérrez does not reject Althusser's point of view out of hand. To the contrary, he recognizes that individuality in its more extreme form, what he calls "individualism," [24] is one of the more salient aspects of contemporary capitalism and present-day thought. It serves as "the point of departure and motive force of economic activity" [25] as well as an "ethical" principle that guides consumer society. In *We Drink from Our Own Wells*, Gutiérrez shows that the cult of excessive individualism has even had an impact on theological thought:

> Individualism operates, in fact, as a filter that makes it possible to "spiritualize" and even volatize what in the Bible are nuanced statements of a social and historical nature. For example, the poor/rich opposition (a social fact) is reduced to the humble/proud opposition (something within the individual). "Passage" through the individual interiorizes, and robs of their historical bite, categories reflective of the objective realities in which individuals and peoples live and die, struggle and assert their faith. [26]

What Gutiérrez intimates is that theology and theologians have all too often abetted capitalism by stressing individuality at the expense of our collective nature. By doing so they have "euphemized" oppression and dulled our awareness of others as brothers and sisters for whom we are responsible. Coopted and content with a cozy niche in the status quo, they have often been conveniently uncritical of the real causes of oppression. In some ways, then, Althusser's analysis of the ideological role of individualism and critique of Christianity is justified.

Gutiérrez, however, does not confuse individualism with individuality. He considers a balanced, socially integrated sense of self indispensable if the exaggerated selfhood of modern capitalism is to be effectively addressed. Whether Christian or Marxist, a person committed to social change must know himself or herself as both a responsible person and member of society. In direct opposition to Althusser Gutiérrez states that:

> Alienation and exploitation as well as the very struggle for liberation from them have ramifications on the personal and psychological planes which it would be dangerous to overlook in the process of constructing a new society and a new man. [27]

An exaggerated sense of the collective is obviously as dangerous as a disproportionate sense of individuality. For Althusserian Marxists the pronoun "I" may border on the obscene, but without a balanced sense of self we run the risk of producing an unbalanced vision of society, be it capitalist or Marxist.

As regards Althusser's criticism of the church, Gutiérrez is quite willing to admit that it has often served as an ideological apparatus:

> In Latin America, the whole "Christian set-up" is made to play a part inside the dominant ideology, which helps to strengthen and affirm a society divided into antagonistic classes. Conservative sectors in fact frequently appeal to Christian ideas to justify the social order which serves their interests and maintains their privileges.[28]

It is an unfortunate but undeniable fact that the church has more often than not spoken for the oppressor rather than for the oppressed. Distorting evangelical concepts, it has preached passivity and other-worldliness, and so abetted exploitation. Gutiérrez, however, feels that the church can change. Instead of supporting the status quo it can subvert it. But to do this, it must first make a clear option for the oppressed. In the penultimate chapter of *A Theology of Liberation,* dedicated to ecclesiology, Gutiérrez takes this theme up in response to Althusser's critique of institutional Christianity.

> Understood in this way, the unity of the Church is rightly considered by Althusser as a myth which must disappear if the Church is to be "reconverted" to the service of the workers in the class struggle: "For this to happen," he asserts, "it would be necessary that the myth of the 'Christian community' disappear, for it prevents the recognition of class struggle. One can foresee serious divisions occurring in the Church precisely around the theme of the *recognition* and the *understanding* of social classes and the class struggle, the recognition and the understanding of a reality which is incompatible with the *peculiarly religious* myth of the 'community of the faithful' and the (catholic) universality of the Church." The author [Althusser] does not seem very convinced of the possibility for this "reconversion."[29]

Althusser's skeptical assessment of the the church is based on his experience of French Catholicism, with its close ties to the conservative sector. The sociological and ecclesiastical gap between France and Peru, however, is wide. First of all, most Peruvians, particularly those from the oppressed sector, are consciously Christian. And, as we saw previously, their faith often serves as a critical force in their lives. Secondly, at least until the present, the Peruvian hierarchy has been theologically and politically progressive and has often called for social change as morally imperative.

These facts have clear implications for the church's self-definition and ability to change its socio-political orientation. Thus,

> there are growing numbers of Christians who challenge the mythical notion of the Christian community alluded to by Althusser and who

believe that the authentic unity of the Church necessarily implies the option for the oppressed and exploited of this world.[30]

The church Gutiérrez speaks of is aware that it lives "in a society that is divided and conflictual." Rather than avoiding class conflict, it recognizes that to "participate actively in it"[31] is the only way of overcoming the division and injustice that it fosters. Certainly, his position is borne out by both the Medellín and Puebla documents that call for justice and social reform. As Gutiérrez knows from experience, the church need not be an ideological apparatus. The fundamental question is where and with whom it stands. Althusser's criticism of the church is based on past history and a materialist rejection of faith. Gutiérrez's understanding of the church is based on what it is becoming and hopefully will continue to be.

For Gutiérrez the danger of Althusserian Marxism is that it tends towards a type of exclusivist "neopositivism" that rejects concepts "which fail to fit within his restricted vision of science."[32] Among the most important of these concepts is utopia, which Althusser considers a form of idealism incompatible with a "scientific" reading of Marx. Gutiérrez finds this posture totally unacceptable, as he points out in *A Theology of Liberation:*

> The rigidity of this position and the consignment of every utopian element to ideology prevents seeing the profound unity of the work of Marx and consequently duly understanding his capacity for inspiring a radical and permanent revolutionary praxis.[33]

As we have often seen, Gutiérrez synthetically links political commitment and faith by means of utopia. Without a sense of and belief in the future, political action loses its meaning and liberation becomes an empty term.

Fixated by his quest to recast Marxism in a "scientific" mold, Althusser loses sight of the real force that moves society — human beings. Many facets of his analysis of ideology and capitalism are interesting and possibly true, but ultimately his interpretation of Marxism is elitist and pessimistic. Not surprisingly, there are practically no references to the poor in Althusser's works. They are considered too contaminated by capitalism to effectively change society. But who then struggles to overcome oppression? Presumably elite left-wing cadres equipped with a "scientific" knowledge of Marx. Ever patient, Gutiérrez takes Althusser seriously because of his influential role in Latin America. But Gutiérrez knows full well that Althusser's thought is an aberration that must be refuted. As well as badly underestimating the revolutionary power of faith, it fails to recognize the intelligence and thirst for liberation that moves the poor forward in history.

Gramsci

Antonio Gramsci's fame could be justified on the basis of one succinct but remarkably powerful sentence he wrote: "To tell the truth is revolutionary."[34] His reputation, however, is the result of years of committed labor to contextualize and implement Marx's ideas in his native Italy.[35] His writings have been influential in Latin America for nearly sixty years thanks to one of their earliest proponents, José Carlos Mariátegui. During his exile in Europe from 1919 to 1923, Mariátegui spent considerable time in Italy, where he began a systematic analysis of his writings. As Liss notes in his study of Latin American Marxism, the two theorists shared common presuppositions about culture and religion as well as the need for contextualizing political theory.

> They both believed in the role of intellectuals in controlling the revolution. Mariátegui, like Gramsci, felt that for him politics included both philosophy and religion. They also agreed that successful socialist revolution occurs only when Marxist theory is attuned to national conditions, that one deals with regional or national problems, often through popular culture, en route to internationalism.[36]

Presumably the affinity between the two analysts was also stimulated by the common characteristics of their respective countries. In the 1920s Peru and Italy both had large rural populations broken into provincial and linguistic pockets that hampered political and economic integration. Both authors had to come to terms with unique economic and cultural situations unlike those of industrialized Europe where the rural population was in decline. Because Peru still has a large, culturally independent rural population, Gutiérrez has been able to use Gramsci's insights with special effectiveness. The latter's analyses of peasant society, culture, and religion constantly surface in his theology.

Gramsci's approach to Marxism differs radically from Althusser's. His was an inclusive interpretation rather than exclusive. Although he considered Marx's writings as foundational and indispensable for revolutionary social change, he realized they had to be translated in terms of the history and culture of a given country. Otherwise they risked becoming an abstract, materialist "metaphysics." Gramsci consequently studied the religious and cultural history of Italy in great detail. In this section and the next on Bloch, then, we are dealing with Marxist theorists who approached society with few *a prioris*. They felt an affinity to peasants and workers and realized their experience was far more important than erudite theory in mobilizing people for social change.

Although it may be purely coincidental, the first note in *A Theology of Liberation* draws on Gramsci's thinking about the need for an inclusive approach to social reality that respects the experience of the poor. Setting out his thesis that there is a theological "outline...present in *all believers* — and more so in every Christian community,"[37] Gutiérrez is actually paraphrasing Gramsci's words, of course not about theology per se, but about the wisdom of ordinary people:

What Antonio Gramsci said of philosophy is also true of theology: It is necessary to destroy the widely-held prejudice that philosophy is something extremely difficult because it is the intellectual activity proper to a certain category of scientific specialists or professional and systematic philosophers. It is necessary, therefore, to demonstrate first that all men are "philosophers," establishing the parameters and characteristics of this "spontaneous philosophy" proper to everyman.[38]

What Gramsci proposes is that every human being has a certain sense of his or her own being, a unique self-knowledge or *autocomprensión,* which is a functional sort of philosophy. Rarely verbalized, it is nonetheless a sophisticated system of thought based on observation and collective experience. It is a working philosophy with which people structure and give meaning to their lives. Gutiérrez feels that the same process occurs along theological lines. People develop theological notions of God, personal and collective moralities, and definitions of life. These ideas are distinct from the official philosophies and theologies of the dominant sector and institutional church. Often glibly dismissed as "folklore, they nonetheless reflect the deeper values of ordinary" people.

As we saw in the first chapter, Gutiérrez draws on the Gramscian concept of contradiction to explain the growing critical consciousness of the poor in Third World nations. Aware that the promises of economic well-being and a meaningful life transmitted by the dominant sector's ideological apparatuses do not match experience, many of the poor have become skeptical of capitalism itself. They realize, for instance, that the hype of consumerism is a chimera meant to mollify their resistance to an unjust, exploitative socio-economic system. Such critical consciousness helps the poor to understand both the economic and human gap that separates them from the dominant sector. More importantly, it has stimulated a new sense among the oppressed sector of its uniqueness and need to shape society in a way consonant with its own "philosophy" in the Gramscian sense of the word. As Gutiérrez puts it:

> ... political consciousness is sharpened when the contradiction grows between an increasing aspiration to secure effective freedom and justice, and the existence of a social order which claims to recognize freedom and justice in law, but in reality denies them in countless ways to social classes, entire peoples and racial minorities. Hence the revolutionary, militant search for the right conditions for the construction of a free, just society, and the attitude of critical suspicion towards any ideological argument designed to conceal a situation of cruelty and discord.[39]

However, people's values and beliefs become effective political catalysts only when they are coupled with a critical "observation of historical events" that leads "to the discovery of their meaning."[40] Consequently, a solid knowledge of the way society works is an indispensable ingredient in the "revolutionary search" Gutiérrez calls for. What might be called "popular philosophy" needs hard social analysis if it is to have any real effect.

Using a famous Gramscian term that we have already seen on numerous occasions, he feels that the acquisition and dissemination of this critical knowledge among the oppressed is the special domain of the "organic intellectual." In *The Power of the Poor in History* he sketches the main characteristics of this indispensable individual in theological terms:

> Theological reasoning is an effort on the part of concrete persons to form and think out their faith in determinate circumstances, to plan activities and make interpretations that play a role in the real-life occurrences and confrontations of a given society. The theologian does not work in some kind of ahistorical limbo. His or her reflection has a milieu, starts from material bases, addresses us from a precise location, speaks the word of the Lord to us in the vernacular. This leads us, where the theology of liberation is concerned, to view the theologian as Gramsci does: as an "organic intellectual" — organically linked to the popular undertaking of liberation.[41]

The "organic intellectual," whether theologian or political organizer, is an expert in the "real-life occurrences" of society. Yet his or her expertise is not meant to provide impartial analyses. The "organic intellectual" is a person passionately yet intelligently committed to the struggle for justice. She or he walks with the poor as a person skilled in expressing their collective wisdom. The finality of that wisdom is to sustain a vision of integral liberation. Its practical reflection is seen in knowledgeable political action.

In Gutiérrez's view, one of the organic intellectual's primary tasks is to help the oppressed understand both their strengths and weaknesses. The beliefs that sustain them as well as the ideological values that oppress them must be pulled apart and analyzed. This is an on-going process meant to provide people with the critical insights they need to act in a politically effective manner.

> The situation of oppression and exploitation under which these peoples labor is well known. But it is known in general terms. It should now be subjected to a close examination in its precise, current forms. Nothing can replace a serious, scientific knowledge of the nature of the exploitation that the popular masses are suffering. It is equally urgent that we be able to differentiate between various strata and groups within the popular masses — that we come to recognize which are more advanced and which are more backward, both in terms of their basic relationship to the productive process, and in terms of

their potential for mobilization (in function of their experiences with social struggle, for instance).[42]

The task Gutiérrez describes above entails a type of disciplined, strategic analysis of society meant to facilitate the political action of the oppressed. They need information about how classes interrelate, their role in economic production, their own debilities, and those of the dominant sector in order effectively to challenge and transform the status quo. In short, they require political "self-knowledge," which necessitates taking a hard look at themselves and judging their cohesion and political will. The organic intellectual's task is to facilitate this process.

As Gutiérrez and the studies done by the Las Casas Center demonstrate, as well as being exploited, the poor are often "partially penetrated" or coopted by the dominant sector's ideology. The concept of partial penetration is drawn from Gramsci's writings. Although less than flattering, this fact must be dealt with in such a way that the oppressed can come to terms with their own liabilities. There can be no doubt that that dominant ideology creates fear and passivity. As Gutiérrez observes, many of the poor try to "move up the social ladder in search of individual, selfish solutions to their problems." Yet he is convinced that "people's real will"[43] is evident in their desire for social change.

Articulating and giving force to the "people's real will" is one of the organic intellectual's primary tasks. Echoing Gramsci's ideas, Gutiérrez sees the organic intellectual as a catalyst who helps sustain the movement of the oppressed toward liberation.

> One must also see to it that these classes create the objective conditions in which they may begin the struggle for their rights, begin actually to take power in a society that has refused to recognize them as human beings at all. In the struggle, the masses will come to an awareness that they are a social class, that they may be the agents of a revolution, that they may go forth and build a different society. Their revolutionary potential is something to be cultivated and organized, with a view to concrete efficaciousness in history.[44]

Thus, the organic intellectual is more than a theoretician versed in the oppressed classes' values and culture. He or she is also a tactician adept at planning and strategizing. Like Gramsci, Gutiérrez is aware that social change does not happen willy-nilly. It requires forethought, organization, and intelligent action — these are the important elements or "objective conditions" necessary for social change. The organic intellectual's task is to provide these indispensable ingredients and make them mesh with the aspirations of the oppressed.

Despite Gutiérrez's admiration for Gramsci both as a thinker and political activist, he does not slavishly reproduce the latter's ideas. He reshapes them according to his context. This is a pattern characteristic of Gutiérrez: he is adept at assimilating the best and most usable facets of another person's ideas, but he never falls victim to uncritical adulation. He can accept Gramsci's observations on culture, religion, and the need for organic intellectuals to articulate the vision of the poor, yet he filters out the latter's Marxist bias. This tendency can be explained in two ways. First, Gutiérrez is gifted with an agile intellect that allows him to extrapolate what is most cogent and useful in a given theory while leaving behind secondary considerations, such as Gramsci's materialism. Equally important, however, is his commitment to his own people, which serves as a criterion and filter. Ideas that advance the cause of liberation are incorporated into his theology. Those that do not are left out.

Bloch

Gutiérrez uses the insights of Gramsci on culture and religion to better understand the self-consciousness of the ordinary Peruvians and the need for a political agenda that arises from their self-perception. This long-term concern with the deeper quality of their lives has helped him appreciate a crucially important and powerful facet of their collective existence; despite day-to-day oppression the poor maintain an abiding hope in the future and their hope is something more than a dream. It is a *gestalt,* a powerful set of images, words, and gestures that sustains them in the present and directs them toward the future.

The term Gutiérrez employs to encapsulate the multi-dimensionality of this hope is "utopia." Unfortunately, due to the rigidity of their beliefs and lack of contact with ordinary people, some Marxists and Christians have overlooked the importance of this concept. In Gutiérrez's theology, however, utopia plays an indispensable role. As the Spanish theologian Miguel Manzanera has pointed out, Gutiérrez uses the notion of utopia "in order to correct the dogmatism and pragmatism of communist totalitarianism and the political conservatism of reactionary Christianity associated with traditional circles."[45] Gutiérrez goes beyond such simplistic thinking. Caught up in their respective "orthodoxies," both positions suffer from self-inflicted myopia and their vision of life ultimately proves destructive. The only way to avoid the dangers of both left-wing and right-wing extremism is to listen to the pulse of the lives oppressed peoples. There Gutiérrez hears a rhythm that mocks both the materialism of Marxists and the backward-looking brittleness of conservative Christians.

Gutiérrez turns to a number of theorists to flesh out his understanding of hope, but the most important is Ernst Bloch. None of the social analysts who have influenced Gutiérrez are as difficult to categorize as Bloch. A Marxist and atheist, he was intrigued by the deeper currents of the Judeo-Christian tradition. In it he saw a powerful force that gave a special continuity and meaning to people's lives. He analyzed the course of Western history and saw running through it a vision of the future that both held it together and pushed it forward. The term he used for this phenomenon was "utopia,"[46] basically a synonym for hope. Although he found belief in God impossible, he was intrigued by faith and respectful of those who adhered to it.

Bloch's unimaginative and inflexible Marxist associates were less than enthusiastic about his ideas. He was officially expelled from the Communist party, later readmitted, voluntarily withdrew, and then reentered. In the course of his varied career he produced a number of works, the most important of which is *Das Prinzip Hoffnung*, which can be translated as "The Hope Principle." This multi-volume treatise is undoubtedly the definitive treatment of utopia. Although it is not easy reading, *Das Prinzip Hoffnung* has had a profound impact on both social analysis and modern theology. As well as having influenced Gutiérrez, it is also frequently cited by political theologians such as Metz and Moltmann.

In *A Theology of Liberation* Gutiérrez provides a succinct synopsis of Bloch's principal thesis in *Das Prinzip Hoffnung*, which, in many ways, is a synopsis of his own understanding of utopia:

> For Bloch man is he who hopes for and dreams of the future; but it is an active hope which subverts the existing order. He accepts Marx's assertion that "philosophers have only *interpreted* the world in various ways; the point, however, is to change it." He uses as his point of departure what Marx himself, in his first thesis on Feuerbach, asserted had been left out of all materialistic theories: "The chief defect of all hitherto existing materialism — that of Feuerbach included — is that the thing [*Gegenstand*], reality, sensuousness, is conceived only in the form of the object [*Objekt*] or of *contemplation* [*Anschauung*], but not as *human sensuous activity, practice*, not subjectively." Bloch attempts to clarify in his work the meaning of these aspects of revolutionary activity, that is to say, of the practico-critical activity.[47]

As well as being a summary of Bloch's ideas, this passage also says a great deal about certain methodological presuppositions that inform Gutiérrez's theology.

Taking his cue from Bloch, Gutiérrez constantly refers to the "materiality" of social thought, be it political or theological. The meaning of the term is elucidated above; materiality means "sensuous activity, practice." It arises from the deepest aspects of human behavior. Although it is most certainly objective, it is also a "subjective" reality because it is part of people's lives. Utilizing Bloch's ideas, Gutiérrez overcomes the traditional dichotomy between the social and personal characteristics of hope. Although it resides in our hearts and feelings and is thus intangible, hope nonetheless affects the shape and physical quality of our world. This insight taken from Bloch allows Gutiérrez to escape from the vulgar materialism of certain Marxists who cannot bear to discuss questions of subjectivity and individuality, and avoid the idealism of certain Christian theologians who refuse to take society seriously.

Gutiérrez goes on to show precisely how utopic hope functions as a social force. He sketches the foundations of a new socio-theological methodology based on the aspirations of the oppressed. The language Gutiérrez employs here is admittedly difficult, but contending with its complexity provides us with a sense of what might be called the "teleology of hope" that informs his understanding of the finality of liberative praxis.

> Hope is a "daydream" projected into the future; it is the "yet not-conscious" (*Noch-Nicht-Bewusst*), the psychic representation of that which "is not yet" (*Noch-Nicht-Sein*). But this hope seeks to be clear and conscious, a *docta spes*. When that which is "yet not-conscious" becomes a conscious act, it is no longer a state of mind; it assumes a concrete utopic function, mobilizing human action in history. Hope thus emerges as the key to human existence oriented towards the future, because it transforms the present. This ontology of what "is not yet" is dynamic, in contrast to the static ontology of being, which is incapable of planning history.... Bloch brings us into the area of the possibilities of potential being; this allows us to plan history in revolutionary terms.[48]

Thus, hope, which seems to be only expectation and latency, gives society its forward momentum. It challenges the oppression of the present and calls us to a just, liberated future. Hope sustains existence and gives it meaning despite the most egregious oppression. For Gutiérrez it is "*docta*," that is, wise.

As Gutiérrez mentions above, utopic hope looks at present reality in order to determine the shape of the future. In effect, its chronological point of reference is twofold. It is both "retrospective" and "prospective." In his analysis of Gutiérrez's theology Manzanera provides us with a helpful explanation of what these adjectives mean.

> The retrospective character of utopia is its denunciation of the present "order" to the extent that it is generated by a past characterized by injustice and oppression.
>
> The prospective character [of utopia] is tied to the future with its annunciation of a new order, of a new society, which is still to come, but which exists in the rational, imaginative hope of that which will be.[49]

Thus, utopia links the present and future. It is the dynamic thread that runs through history. It is also a political force since its images of futurity critique the present order and call for a reconstructed society that coincides with our full human potential.

Utopia both denounces and announces. Given the oppression of the poor, their hope for the future inevitably requires that they condemn the present system. This condemnation is radical in the sense that it rejects the values and presuppositions on which the established system of oppression is based:

> Utopia necessarily means a denunciation of the existing order. Its deficiencies are to a large extent the reason for the emergence of a utopia. The repudiation of a dehumanizing situation is an unavoidable aspect of utopia. It is a matter of a complete rejection which attempts to strike at the roots of the evil. This is why utopia is revolutionary and not reformist.[50]

Yet utopia is not mere negativity. By calling for a just social order it motivates opposition to the status quo and sustains the hope of the oppressed.

> But utopia is also an annunciation, an annunciation of what is not yet, but will be; it is the forecast of a different order of things, a new society. It is the field of creative imagination which proposes the alternative values to those rejected. This denunciation is to a large extent made with regard to the annunciation.[51]

In Gutiérrez's view utopia is an all-important source of political action that fosters "a historical plan for a qualitatively different society and . . . the aspiration to establish new social relations."[52] In fact, the criterion for utopic hope is effective, concrete political action. Without it utopia remains "at a purely verbal level and the annunciation will be only an illusion."[53]

Rather than being an abstraction, utopia is a social force intimately tied up with the material, social conditions of life. It lives in the counter-ideological, revolutionary aspirations of the poor for justice and in their desire to shape society according to their needs. In terms of the status quo the utopian hope of the poor is clearly subversive. It aspires to turn exploitation on its head and rewrite history. Gutiérrez is unequivocal on this point: "Utopian thought is taking on, in line with the initial intention, its quality of being subversive to and a driving force of history."[54] Thus, what most of us have been taught by the dominant ideology to view as a mere daydream becomes the stuff of revolutionary change.

As Gutiérrez knows, the utopian hope of the oppressed and the revolutionary praxis it engenders invariably meet opposition. Inevitably, " 'utopianism' clashes with the 'realism' of the oppressor who is incapable of appreciating the kind of historical rationality that springs from the power of the poor."[55] Because the utopian hope of the oppressed threatens the very logic of an oppressive society, it is constantly attacked by ideological mechanisms and ridiculed as an illogical dream.

Expanding on Bloch's ideas, Gutiérrez considers utopia to be the opposite of ideology. The former engenders a sense of possibility and rational political praxis aimed at establishing a just social order. The latter preserves the distorted values of the status quo and "rationalizes" the injustice it propagates.

Ideology does not offer adequate and scientific knowledge of reality, rather it masks it. Ideology does not rise above the empirical, irrational level. Therefore, it spontaneously fulfills a function of preservation of the established order. Therefore, also, ideology tends to dogmatize all that has not succeeded in separating itself from it or has fallen under its influence.... Utopia, however, leads to an authentic and scientific knowledge of reality and to a praxis which transforms what exists.[56]

As Gutiérrez sees it, the so-called rationality of the status quo is nothing more than self-serving logic of an elite whose knowledge is limited to what perpetuates its power. Utopia, on the other hand, looks towards what is deepest in human nature. It is the "theoretical construct which allows us to know social reality and which makes political action efficacious." Ideology creates ignorance and oppression while utopia "constitutes the essence of ... creativity and dynamism."[57]

Beyond a doubt, Gutiérrez's debt to Bloch is profound. The ideas we have examined have deep implications for the way he views the finality of human action, particularly in the political realm. Rather than being a peripheral activity, political praxis informed by utopian hope is at the essence of what it means to be creative and human. Gutiérrez spells this out in theological terms as follows:

Indeed, if human history is above all else an opening to the future, then it is a task, a political occupation, through which man orients and opens himself to the gift which gives history its transcendent meaning: the full and definitive encounter with the Lord and with other men. "To do the truth," as The Gospel says, thus acquires a precise and concrete meaning in terms of the importance of action in Christian life.[58]

The theological import of Gutiérrez's views is obvious: social action is now a *locus theologicus* rather than a noisome activity unrelated to Christian life. If we assent to the vision of human life contained in the gospels, we have no choice but to be actively concerned about the shape of the world we live in. Belief cannot be isolated from daily life or sealed up within itself since it is part of a far more expansive reality that foreshadows the reign of God. At its deepest level, the political activity of the Christian expresses his or her conviction that hope is not an illusion, that it can be made real in the world we inhabit.

The Social Sciences and Gutiérrez's Theology

Given the breadth of Gutiérrez's experience and the number of people who shape his ideas, summarizing the way he employs the social sciences in his theology is a difficult task. An important point to keep in mind is that he uses the social sciences in the broad sense of the term. He employs and mixes together economics, political theory, and even literature, since it too describes the human condition of the poor. He is not fixed on one particular discipline or mode of analysis, but rather concerned to describe adequately the sources of oppression in contemporary society. And this description has a clear purpose: facilitating liberative praxis.

For Gutiérrez Christians cannot turn a blind eye to the forms of suffering that surround them since they embody "death and sin which deny the resurrection."[59] This suffering must be overcome. Christians must scrutinize the societies they live in, grapple with their problems, and, informed and motivated by the gospel, take concrete action to overcome those sinful forces that cause pain and deny life. That, in essence, is what Gutiérrez means by liberative praxis, which is "an option for life, in all its expressions."[60] The liberative praxis of the Christian is his or her way of collaborating with that ultimate utopic and eschatological symbol we call the reign of God. If that collaboration is to be effective it must be grounded in an analytical, even scientific knowledge of society. But analysis is only a tool, a relative means to an absolute end called integral human liberation.

For Gutiérrez theology, as reflection on our lived faith, and social analysis, as disciplined study of the way we live, have a common task. In their respective ways each examines our life in society and suggests a course of action that will address its defects. The knowledge they provide "is linked to transformation,"[61] which is both their source of motivation and criterion of effectiveness. There is no fundamental contradiction between theology and critical analysis or between faith and social action. If faith is to have any real bearing in the world it needs sound analysis and data about society. Likewise, if social action is to appeal to what is deepest and most creative among the poor of Latin America it must come to terms with a people that is both "believing and oppressed."[62] Gutiérrez spells out the consequences of this new relationship:

> The future is in the hands of a faith which does not fear the progress of human learning nor the challenges of social practices, but which lets itself be questioned by them and questions them in return, enriching itself. It is a complex task which takes into account many lines of specialization, philosophical and scientific, without which it is impossible, today, to elaborate a theological process. It takes into

account, among others, those sciences which provide us with instruments enabling us to know the natural world of which we are a part, and particularly of those which allow us to discover our psychological, economic, and social dimensions which militate against justice and fraternity.[63]

Theology and social analysis, then, are meant to enrich each other. What they reveal can help the other come to a fuller, more critical sense of the challenges that are entailed in a radical restructuring of society. Knowing a society's "soul," so to speak, is as important as analyzing the social structures that give that "soul" its particular shape.

Theology and the social sciences, however, do not blend into some type of amalgam. Theology is concerned with the broad sweep of history characterized by a complex mix of human goodness, sinfulness, and the mysterious presence of God in our midst. The focus of the social sciences is more limited. They examine facets of this totality, the bits and pieces that make up the whole. This difference is crucial and Gutiérrez insists that it be kept in mind:

> A central point is this, that theology point to the presence of our relationship with God and the rupture of that relationship with God evident in the very heart of our historical, political, and economic situation — something social analysis can never do. A sociologist will never see that in the very heart of an unjust social reality lies the presence of sin: a rupture with God and others. Furthermore, the indispensable use of a certain type of rationality in theology does not presuppose an uncritical posture or identification with that particular type of rationality. "Theology is not identified with one method of social analysis or one philosophical position about human beings. Theology never employs a certain mode of rational analysis without, in a certain way, changing it."[64]

Thus, to accuse Gutiérrez of overlooking the differences between theology and the social sciences totally misses the mark. Unfortunately, this is precisely what the first Vatican "instruction" on liberation theology does. Gutiérrez is not mentioned by name, but he and other liberation theologians are clearly targeted. The Vatican treatise states that there is a distinct epistemology involved in theology and that confusing it with social analysis, particularly of a Marxist variety, is an erroneous and dangerous move.

Gutiérrez, however, is more than aware of the dangers of uncritically mixing theology and the social sciences. The Roman instruction declares that "critical study is missing from more than one 'theology of liberation,'"[65] since Marxist social analysis is purportedly used without taking stock of the materialist presuppositions that stand behind it. If this accusation is being hurled at Gutiérrez one can only question its aim and accuracy. As far back as 1974 he insisted on the autonomy of theology and realized that it had to employ the insights of the social sciences in an independent way. This is due to the very purpose of theology, elucidating and articulating how we relate to a God present among us. Such a task requires a broader, more inclusive sense of history than that offered by social analysis, Marxist or otherwise.

Having read the social sciences extensively, Gutiérrez knows that they have many limitations. The fact that there are Marxist, neo-Marxist, and empiricist varieties of social research proves that philosophical presuppositions and biases make social research less scientific than certain of its practitioners claim. Precisely for this reason Gutiérrez uses the insights of social theorists selectively and judiciously:

> Beyond a doubt, the use of the social sciences, as is frequently pointed out in our works, is in its "first steps" ... as a scientific effort. As such, the use of the social sciences is far from fixed. Our posture toward their use should be one of discernment, not only because of the incipient characteristics we have pointed out, but also because the fact that they are classified as sciences does not mean that we are dealing with something apodictic or non-debatable. Just the opposite is true.[66]

As Gutiérrez asserts, canonizing the findings of social analysis in general or a specific school of thought as normative for Christians would be a mistake. Such a posture cannot be reconciled with the breadth of the gospel nor with the multi-dimensionality of human experience. Gutiérrez has never been party to the naïve and simplistic thinking Cardinal Ratzinger attributes to liberation theology.

For some critics the fact that Gutiérrez turns to Marxist theorists is problematic in itself. The Vatican instruction goes so far as to attribute the use of Marxist social analysis in liberation theology to an unfortunate "impatience and a desire for results,"[67] apparently characteristic of Third World Christians confronted with injustice. This accusation, however, is easily refuted in Gutiérrez's case. He is hardly prone to impatience, and he has studied Marxist social theory in detail. He is more than capable of distinguishing its true and false points.

Gutiérrez is convinced that certain Marxist social theorists explain facets of contemporary society with special precision. But we should keep in mind that he employs their ideas because they accurately describe social reality, not because of their connection with Marxism. Summarizing Gutiérrez's approach to Marxism, McAfee Brown makes the following observation:

> The importance of an idea lies not in who said it, but in whether or not it accurately describes the world in which we live. If it does

not, we need not take it seriously even if it has been propounded by a theologian; if it does, we must take it seriously even if it has been propounded by a Karl Marx.[68]

Obviously, this does not mean that all of Marx's ideas are correct. Marx suffers from what Gutiérrez and others call "eurocentrism,"[69] and his materialist bias is all too obvious. Many of his theories are either wrong or now outdated. Nonetheless, his ideas and those of other Marxists have had a profound impact in the field of social and economic analysis. As Gutiérrez mentions, references to Marx's ideas "are frequent in the contemporary intellectual world, even in theology."[70] Regardless of what one thinks of this fact it cannot be denied. Furthermore, when they are correctly understood, certain insights from the Marxist tradition give added concreteness to theology. For example, the Marxist emphasis on the centrality of history and necessity for social action on behalf of the poor is certainly not antithetical to Christianity.

Gutiérrez knows full well that every tenet of Marxist theory cannot be reconciled with Christian faith. We have already seen how he responds to the theories of Althusser that threaten a responsible sense of individuality. Even the ideas of more flexible Marxists such as Mariátegui, Gramsci, and Bloch are duly scrutinized. There is no room in Gutiérrez's theological vision for any type of materialism or determinist version of history. He believes too firmly in the reality and power of the Spirit to fall victim to such simplistic thinking. Gutiérrez is quite aware that Marxism is capable of becoming an ideological, anti-evangelical social theory, particularly when it is accepted uncritically. When this is the case it must be rejected in terms of "our faith, our humanist perspective, and also in terms of a sound type of social analysis."[71]

Class Struggle and Liberative Praxis

Of the many themes in Gutiérrez's writings and liberation theology in general none elicits a greater reaction than that of class struggle. Surely it is a powerful concept bound to generate an emotional response, be it positive or negative. For many poor of the Third World the fact that theologians like Gutiérrez speak of class struggle is a sign of hope. It indicates a deeper understanding of their situation and an encouraging commitment to liberation on the part of Christians who previously were either apolitical or conservative.

For certain members of the dominant sector, however, Gutiérrez is a left-wing *agent provocateur* disguised as a Christian. His theology is no theology at all, but a "christianized" front for revolutionary violence. This is proven beyond a doubt since the topic of class struggle appears in his writings. The first document on liberation theology issued by the Vatican is only slightly more kind in its assessment. In the opinion of its author the theme of class struggle discussed by Gutiérrez and other theologians is an extremely dangerous precedent that can lead to the "affirmation of necessary violence" and "political amorality."[72] Theologians who use the concepts are supposedly dupes of Marxism who threaten the integrity of Christian faith.

Putting aside such characterizations and hyperbole, however, the reaction of both the dominant class and certain segments of the institutional church is inaccurate and unjustified. Gutiérrez never equates class struggle with violent revolution. He has spent his life trying to overcome violence, not promote it. He understands class struggle as a moral obligation incumbent on Christians of conscience who are called to follow the standards of ethical behavior set out in Matthew 25. In the paragraphs that follow we shall analyze in detail what Gutiérrez actually means by the term. It should become clear early on that Gutiérrez uses the concept of class struggle in a specifically Christian way quite distinct from the Marxist tradition.

To grasp properly what Gutiérrez means by class struggle we need to take a critical look at the society he lives in. Discussing the concept abstractly will only lead to confusion and mistakes.[73] As we have seen, Peruvian society is highly stratified. Social classes exist in any capitalist society, but in Peru and other Third World countries the breach between rich and poor is an immense chasm. Class stratification in Peruvian society is much more than a question of a person's income. It is a question of what people eat, believe, and how they are treated as human beings. Class stratification is clearly more than an economic problem. It is a fundamental social and moral issue. It speaks of false and destructive social values that pit one person against another. Class stratification allows a small but powerful elite to live off the bitter fruits of this conflict.

Gutiérrez has been accused of equating class struggle with the abolition of economic differences between the rich and poor, thus propagating a type of economist communism.[74] Such an assertion is totally inaccurate. In an important article, Gutiérrez states that we "must bear in mind the *non-economic aspects* of confrontation between social groups." He goes on to reject any analytical perspective that reduces class conflict to the economic realm as "totally foreign to my perspective in *A Theology of Liberation*."[75] Although he frequently calls the struggle between oppressors and oppressed a "class struggle," he never uses the phrase in a vulgar, materialistic sense. It is not simply a question of economic competition between the wealthy and poor or a tactical means to a political end, but a struggle about definitions of life and the right of the poor to shape their own history. As such, class struggle is an eminently theological concern that speaks of the poor's aspiration for full humanity as mandated by the gospel and even the social teaching of the Catholic Church.

Gutiérrez is convinced that capitalistic ideology has pushed Latin America to a type of "liminal chaos"[76] that is destroying generations of people.

He goes so far as to liken the effects of contemporary capitalism to those of the ideology of the Nazis.[77] The distorted values of both systems have caused countless deaths. For Gutiérrez class struggle is an ethical obligation that flows out of his "conviction of the radical incompatibility of evangelical demands with an unjust and alienating society."[78] It is a struggle on behalf of the deeper truths of life that the ideology of the oppressors distort and destroy.

Gutiérrez insists that class stratification be understood as an inevitable result of the way capitalism works. The fact that there is an immense gap between the rich and poor has nothing to do with luck, intelligence, or moral bearing. Nor are the poor temporarily "marginalized" as advocates of the development theory claim. Their marginalization is an integral aspect of the current system and corresponds "to its historic logic and development."[79] In Gutiérrez's view, Latin Americans live in the midst of "social conflict that we do not want ... but cannot deny."[80] And the only way to effectively overcome class conflict is to work for a society in which social classes disappear. Thus,

> those who speak of class struggle do not "advocate" it — as some would say — in the sense of creating it out of nothing by an act of (bad) will. What they do is to recognize a fact and contribute to an awareness of that fact. And there is nothing more certain than a fact. To ignore it is to deceive and to be deceived and moreover to deprive oneself of the necessary means of truly and radically eliminating this condition — that is, by moving towards a classless society. Paradoxically, what the groups in power call "advocating" class struggle is really an expression of a will to abolish its causes, to abolish them, not to cover them over, to eliminate the appropriation by a few of the wealth created by the work of many and not to make lyrical calls to social harmony.[81]

The calls for "social harmony" Gutiérrez refers to are part of the classic ideological repertoire of the dominant sector. The poor are told they are socially equal to the rich because under capitalism everyone supposedly possesses the same economic rights. With patience and hard work anyone can acquire wealth and security. Yet believing such patently ideological myths only results in a "society of superficial and false reconciliation and equality."[82] Perhaps a few "lucky" poor will manage to "make it" at the expense of their fellows, but the underlying pathogen of classism will not be eradicated.

For Gutiérrez the purpose of class struggle is to root out class stratification. It is not a type of social warfare, but part of a struggle to create an egalitarian society in which every person's worth and rights are respected, not because he or she is rich or powerful, but because of a shared human identity.

To "advocate" class struggle, therefore, is to reject a situation in which there are oppressed and oppressors. But it is a rejection without deceit or cowardliness; it is to recognize that the fact exists and that it profoundly divides men, in order to be able to attack it at its roots and thus create the conditions of an authentic human community. To build a just society today necessarily implies the active and conscious participation in the class struggle that is occurring before our eyes.[83]

In Gutiérrez's opinion "advocating class struggle" is ultimately an act of honesty and optimism. It is a sign of hope that human beings can live in a realistic and just way without the oppression and class stratification that now afflict them. It is a creative effort of exploited peoples to take away the oppressors' system of oppression and assume their role in society and history as persons of dignity.

Like it or not, there is no way one can straddle the fence in a situation of class stratification. Either one sides with the oppressed or with the oppressors. A fundamental decision has to be made, even by the Christian who believes in universal love. Despite the fact that many in the institutional church preach social "non-alignment," such a posture is impossible. Drawing from the ideas of Girardi, Gutiérrez unequivocally states his own position:

Neutrality is impossible. It is not a question of admitting or denying a fact which confronts us; rather it is a question of which side we are on. The so-called "interclassist doctrine," writes Girardi in a well-known article on this question, "is in fact very classist: it reflects the point of view of the dominant class." When the Church rejects the class struggle, it is objectively operating as a part of the prevailing system. By denying the existence of social division, this system seeks to perpetuate the division on which are based the privileges of its beneficiaries. It is a classist option, deceitfully camouflaged by a purported equality before the law.[84]

In practical terms, neutrality only perpetuates injustice. It sanctions the status quo with silence. In theological terms, tolerating class stratification effectively denies that the "Gospel announces the love of God for all people and calls us to love as he loves."[85]

Gutiérrez insists that class struggle, as a struggle for justice and human dignity, is totally consonant with Christian love. In fact, it is an effective application of Christian principles in a classist society. Its purpose is to give life to the oppressed and save oppressors from their own violence.

The universality of Christian love is only an abstraction unless it becomes concrete history, process, conflict; it is arrived at only through particularity. To love all men does not mean avoiding confrontations;

it does not mean preserving a fictitious harmony. Universal love is that which in solidarity with the oppressed seeks also to liberate the oppressors from their own power, from their ambition, and from their selfishness. . . . But this cannot be achieved except by resolutely opting for the oppressed, that is, by combating the oppressive class. It must be a real and effective combat, not hate.[86]

Motivated by love, the Christian involved in class struggle witnesses to human equality and the dignity of the poor that the dominant system denies. He or she contradicts the ideological values of the rich by standing with those whom they oppress and despise.

Given the oppression of the dominant system, it is morally incumbent on Christians to struggle for a new society. The suffering of the poor cannot be tolerated. Their humanity and worth cannot be sacrificed for the sake of a privileged few. The situation of oppression and poverty characteristic of Peru and other Third World countries is an affront to Christian values, an outrageous denial of everything the gospel stands for. Thus, to participate in class struggle becomes a statement of principles for the contemporary Christian. As Gutiérrez sees it, class struggle is "a rejection of every kind of complicity with executioners, a straightforward solidarity, an uncompromising denunciation of evil, a prayer of commitment."[87]

As he points out, this is not a novel view concocted by certain theologians. Rather, it is the position of the institutional church itself. Analyzing the writings of various popes, he feels that "the affirmation of class struggle is found in the writings of the Magisterium,"[88] many of which are of recent origin. In his 1984 article in *Páginas* he makes frequent references to *Laborem Exercens,* where John Paul II speaks of class struggle, devoid of any hateful element, as a way of "initiating frank discussion based on a love for justice."[89] Thus, although many of his right-wing ecclesiastical critics would like to deny it, there is a remarkable parallel between the social teaching of the Catholic Church and Gutiérrez's understanding of class struggle. This is not an accident but rather the result of careful analysis of recent encyclicals.[90]

Class struggle for Gutiérrez is clearly positive and creative. It is an expression of Christian hope and belief in the fundamental unity of all people, which classism denies. Class struggle is not class warfare. Its purpose is not to vanquish the oppressor only to create new and more insidious forms of oppression. Gutiérrez is quite aware of how awry certain Marxist revolutions have gone. He knows full well that the "dictatorship of the proletariat" is a destructive illusion. To insinuate that he and other liberation theologians are naïve about the dangers of this Marxist doctrine, as the first Vatican instruction does, is to bring unfounded charges.[91] Class struggle has nothing to do with class hatred. Its purpose is solidarity and justice, not destruction and division. Gutiérrez is adamant on this point:

When we speak of becoming cognizant of social conflict, and even when we speak of the fact of class struggle, ... we affirm the permanent demand of Christian love. We recall, in this way, a basic demand of the Gospel: loving one's enemies. Which is to say, the present painful situation which forces us to see some as our adversaries, does not absolve us from loving them, quite to the contrary. For this reason, when we speak of social opposition, we are referring to social groups, classes, races, and cultures, but not to persons.[92]

As we have already seen, class struggle is meant to fight against the oppressors' power and blindness. It is meant to disarm those who wield destructive social power in the name of an ideological, sinful social system. Class struggle calls the oppressors to conversion. But it does not and may not threaten them with hatred or death without contradicting its own principles and purpose.

Gutiérrez knows full well that class struggle is not a cataclysmic event or revolution of a few days duration. It is a long and complex process that demands political maturity and analytical ability. It is above all a collective undertaking that requires multiple talents and personalities. Gutiérrez likens class struggle to the Exodus, a long process in which oppressed people forged a new self-identity through common labor and a united spirit. Like the oppressed Jews in Egypt, the poor of Latin America are learning that "to struggle against misery and exploitation and to build a just society is already to be part of the saving action, which is moving toward its complete fulfillment."[93] As in the Exodus, it is often difficult to measure progress and people will often be tempted to turn back. Leaving Egypt and struggling against classism have never been easy. But there is progress measured in small but significant steps. Obviously it is crucial that the poor remember that they are not alone. Rather, as Gutiérrez points out time and again, they must be aware that their God walks with them visible in their sisters and brothers.[94]

NOTES

1. Gutiérrez, *The Power of the Poor in History* (Maryknoll, N.Y.: Orbis Books, 1983), p. 192.

2. See Gutiérrez, "Teología y ciencias sociales," *Páginas* 11 (September 1984), pp. 4–15. To my knowledge this important article has yet to be translated into English.

3. Gutiérrez and Shaull, *Liberation and Change,* ed. Ronald H. Stone (Atlanta: John Knox, 1977), p. 30.

4. Gutiérrez, *A Theology of Liberation* (Maryknoll, N.Y.: Orbis Books, 1973), p. 29.

5. Ibid., p. 67.

6. Miguel Manzanera, *Teología y salvación en la obra de Gustavo Gutiérrez* (Bilbao: University of Deusto, 1978), p. 136.

7. Gutiérrez and Shaull, p. 31.
8. Ibid.
9. Ibid.
10. Gustavo Gutiérrez, "Liberation, Theology and Proclamation," in *Concilium* 96, *The Mystical and Political Dimension of the Christian Faith*, ed. Claude Geffré and Gustavo Gutiérrez (New York: Herder and Herder, 1974), p. 61.
11. Gutiérrez, *A Theology of Liberation*, p. 284, note 51.
12. Gutiérrez and Shaull, p. 80.
13. Gutiérrez, *A Theology of Liberation*, p. 29.
14. Ibid., p. 10.
15. Ibid., p. 9.
16. Ibid., p. 30.
17. Gutiérrez, *A Theology of Liberation*, pp. 97 note 40, 249 note 121, and 277.
18. Ibid., p. 97, note 40.
19. Althusser's success is variously rated by his critics. The British neo-Marxist historian E. P. Thompson decimates his ideas. In his opinion Althusser's "thought is the child of economic determinism ravished by theoreticist idealism." See Thompson's work *The Poverty of Theory and Other Essays* (New York and London: Monthly Review Press, 1978), p. 12.
20. Further discussion of the problems posed for Christians by Althusser and the variety of Marxism he represents can be found in René Coste's work *Marxism and Christian Faith* (Maryknoll, N.Y.: Orbis Books, 1985).
21. Louis Althusser, "Ideology and Ideological State Apparatuses" in *Lenin and Philosophy* (New York and London: Monthly Review Press, 1971), p. 171.
22. According to Althusser the primary ideological apparatuses in contemporary society are religion, education, the nuclear family, the legal system, most political parties, trade unions, the mass media, and cultural institutions. In short, almost every public institution in capitalist society functions as a medium for ideological indoctrination. See "Ideology and Ideological State Apparatuses," pp. 141ff.
23. Ibid., pp. 163, 162. This and the following paragraph are a synopsis and interpretation of Althusser's basic thesis in "Ideology and Ideological State Apparatuses." His arguments are complex and treating them so summarily hardly does them justice.
24. Gutiérrez and Shaull, p. 31.
25. Gutiérrez, *The Power of the Poor*, p. 174.
26. Gutiérrez, *We Drink from Our Own Wells: The Spiritual Journey of a People* (Maryknoll, N.Y.: Orbis Books, and Melbourne: Dove Communications, 1984), p. 15.
27. Gutiérrez, *A Theology of Liberation*, p. 31.
28. Gutiérrez, *Concilium* 96: p. 73.
29. Gutiérrez. *A Theology of Liberation*, p. 277.
30. Ibid.
31. Ibid., p. 278.
32. Manzanera, p. 142.
33. Gutiérrez, *A Theology of Liberation*, p. 249, note 121.
34. Antonio Gramsci, *Il materialismo storico e la filosofia di Benedetto Croce* (Turin: Einaudi, 1971), p. xvii. The translation of the title can be rendered as "Historical Materialism and the Philosophy of Benedetto Croce."
35. The bulk of Gramsci's theoretical writing is contained in the *Prison Notebooks*. A good English rendition is available under the following title: *Selections from the Prison Notebooks of Antonio Gramsci*, ed. and trans. Quintin Hoare and Geoffrey Nowell Smith (New York: International Publishers, 1971). The *Prison Notebooks* are notoriously difficult to interpret since, as the title indicates, they were written while Gramsci was being held a prisoner by the fascists. Because his writings had to pass through a censor, they are often cryptic.
36. Sheldon B. Liss, *Marxist Thought in Latin America* (Berkeley: University of California Press, 1984), p. 132.

Marxism, Social Science, and Class Struggle

113

37. Gutiérrez, *A Theology of Liberation*, p. 3.
38. Ibid., p. 15, note 1.
39. Gustavo Gutiérrez, "Liberation Movements and Theology," in *Concilium* 93, *Jesus Christ and Human Freedom*, ed. Edward Schillebeeckx and Bas van Iersel (New York: Herder and Herder, 1974), p. 135.
40. Gutiérrez, *A Theology of Liberation*, p. 13.
41. Gutiérrez, *The Power of the Poor*, p. 212.
42. Ibid., p. 97.
43. Ibid.
44. Ibid.
45. Manzanera, p. 140.
46. A readable analysis of Bloch's understanding of utopia can be found in Gregory Baum's work *Religion and Alienation: A Sociological Reading of Religion* (New York: Paulist Press, 1975), pp. 266–294. As Baum points out, Bloch differentiates between utopias that are unreal, irrational, and ultimately ideological and those that, based on rationality, speak of possible, although yet to be realized, social orders. Well aware of these distinctions, Gutiérrez views true utopias as catalytic visions that give rise to effective, well thought out political projects. As important as utopia is, however, Gutiérrez does not absolutize it. It too must be critiqued in light of evangelical principles. As we shall see in the next chapter, the critical assessment of utopic hope is a constant task of the Christian community.
47. Gutiérrez, *A Theology of Liberation*, p. 216.
48. Ibid.
49. Manzanera, p. 142.
50. Gutiérrez, *A Theology of Liberation*, p. 233.
51. Ibid.
52. Ibid., p. 232.
53. Ibid., p. 234.
54. Ibid., p. 232.
55. Gutiérrez, *The Power of the Poor*, p. 81.
56. Gutiérrez, *A Theology of Liberation*, p. 235.
57. Ibid., p. 234.
58. Ibid., p. 10.
59. Gutiérrez, "Teología y ciencias sociales," p. 6.
60. Ibid.
61. Gutiérrez and Shaull, p. 80.
62. As quoted in James R. Brockman, "The Prophetic Role of the Church in Latin America," *The Christian Century* 100 (October 19, 1983): p. 934.
63. Gutiérrez and Shaull, p. 81.
64. Gutiérrez, "Teología y ciencias sociales, " p. 10. The quotations are from a series of conferences Gutiérrez gave at a CELAM meeting in 1974 held in Bogotá. The texts cited are found in the "Praxis de liberación, teología y evangelización," in *Liberación: diálogos en el CELAM* (Bogotá: CELAM, 1974), pp. 229–230, 88–89 respectively.
65. "Instruction on Certain Aspects of the 'Theology of Liberation,' from the Congregation for the Doctrine of the Faith," *Origins* 15 (April 17, 1986), p. 199.
66. Gutiérrez, "Teología y ciencias sociales," p. 6.
67. "Instruction on Certain Aspects of the 'Theology of Liberation,'" p. 199.
68. Robert McAfee Brown, *Makers of Contemporary Theology: Gustavo Gutiérrez* (Atlanta: John Knox Press, 1980), p. 38.
69. Gutiérrez, "Teología y ciencias sociales," p. 7.
70. Ibid.
71. Ibid., p. 8.
72. Instruction on Certain Aspects of the 'Theology of Liberation,'" p. 200.
73. To venture a personal opinion, this is precisely what the first Vatican Document on liberation theology does. Consequently its observations are flawed.

114 Marxism, Social Science, and Class Struggle

74. This generalized accusation is made in the first document on liberation theology issued in 1985. See page 203, paragraph 11.
75. Gutiérrez, "Teología y ciencias sociales," p. 11.
76. Ibid., p. 14.
77. Ibid.
78. Gutiérrez, A Theology of Liberation, p. 145.
79. Vidales and Kudó, Práctica religiosa y proyecto histórico: hipótesis para un estudio de la religiosidad popular en América Latina (Lima: Centro de Estudios y Publicaciones, 1975), p. 46.
80. Gutiérrez, "Teología y ciencias sociales," p. 10.
81. Gutiérrez, A Theology of Liberation, p. 274.
82. Ibid.
83. Ibid.
84. Ibid., p. 275.
85. Ibid.
86. Ibid., pp. 275–276.
87. Gutiérrez, We Drink from Our Own Wells, p. 23.
88. Gutiérrez, "Teología y ciencias sociales," p. 12.
89. Ibid. Gutiérrez is citing the Spanish version of Laborem Exercens, paragraph 115.
90. In a recent interview in Pastoral Andina Gutiérrez points to the basic affirmation of liberation theology evident in the "Instruction on Christian Freedom and Liberation." This second document issued in the name of the Congregation for the Doctrine of the Faith was obviously crafted in close consultation with Pope John Paul II, since his theological "style" is present throughout the text. It is more positive and affirming than the first instruction and devoid of hyperbole. Gutiérrez sees it as "opening a new stage in the discussion of liberation theology . . . which promises to be more positive and fertile" than in the past. See "Entrevista a Gustavo Gutiérrez: La iglesia y el anuncio del evangelio en el momento actual" in Pastoral Andina 54 (March–April 1986): pp. 9–13.
91. See "Instruction on Certain Aspects of the 'Theology of Liberation,'" p. 200.
92. Gutiérrez, "Teología y ciencias sociales," p. 14.
93. Gutiérrez, A Theology of Liberation, p. 159.
94. This point has been stressed with great poignancy in Gutiérrez's more recent works, especially We Drink from Our Own Wells and On Job. These books study the relationship between the spirituality of contemporary Christians and the challenge of class struggle.

Chapter 5

A Theological Resumé: Society, Jesus, and the Christian Community

Paradoxically, the great utopians have been great realists. They have an extraordinary comprehension of the time and place in which they are writing and deliver themselves of penetrating reflections on socio-economic, scientific, or emotional conditions of their moment in history. They have discovered truths that other men have only vaguely sensed or have refused to recognize. The utopian often emerges as a man with a deeper understanding of the drift of his society than the hardheaded problem-solvers with their noses to the grindstone of the present, blind to potentiality.

— *Frank E. Manuel and Fritzie P. Manuel*[1]

There can be little doubt that Gustavo Gutiérrez has had one overriding purpose — to study, explain, and strengthen the "potentiality" of the poor, and his theology is essentially that potentiality expressed in written form. It is a statement of solidarity with the poor, a protest at their oppression, and an affirmation of the invincibility of their God-given hope.

Gutiérrez's theology is a mixture of feeling and analysis guided by a vision of what it means to be a Christian in a world sadly characterized by systemic oppression. It is a theology of experience, his own and that of the poor, along a long and sinuous road towards liberation. His theological vision has constantly expanded. This is obvious in his written works. *A Theology of Liberation* and *We Drink from Our Own Wells* are different. There is a thread of continuity running between them, but the weave is different.

The shift in emphasis in Gutiérrez's writings is due to the fact that he does not see theology as a set of unchanging truths, but rather a lived reflection on the Christian community's experience of the gospel. It is meant to make people's faith "more radical and clear."[2] It is experiential, but nevertheless a type of "rational knowledge"[3] that must be expressed

115

cogently. Like any systematic theologian Gutiérrez has spent considerable time analyzing the two central symbols of Christian faith: Jesus and the community of believers we call the church.

For Gutiérrez the person and message of Jesus and the life of the Christian community are closely bound together. The community of believers embodies his spirit by preaching that message so central to his life — the advent of God's reign. Like Jesus the Christian community incarnates a life-giving symbol, not outside of history but within it. It proclaims the possibility of salvation despite sin and oppression. As Gutiérrez sees it, the task of the Christian community is to announce *and* embody the words of Paul in Galatians 5:18, namely, that "for freedom Christ has set us free." The Christian community audaciously proclaims that we must "not submit again to the yoke of slavery" but rather live freely and fashion history in accord with Jesus' vision of liberation. It is consequently "anti-ideological." It is a historical countersign that denounces oppression and announces the utopic symbol of God's reign.

For Gutiérrez both Jesus and the Christian community are historical realities. This may seem all too obvious, but there has been a tendency in traditional theology to "hypostatize" Jesus and the church. Supposedly beyond mundane history, Jesus has been turned into an icon removed from ordinary existence. Likewise, the church has been portrayed as a foreshadowing of the "heavenly kingdom" to be ushered in at the end of time. Such abstract christology and ecclesiology are hardly innocuous since they dull the cutting edge of Jesus' words and turn the church into an otherworldly bastion that provides people with the deceptive solace of heavenly compensation. As he points out in *A Theology of Liberation*, abstractions of this sort are incompatible with the incarnation that is a sign of God's presence in history.

> Since God has become man, humanity, every man, history, is the living temple of God. The "pro-fane," that which is located outside the temple, no longer exists.[4]

Thus Jesus and the Christian community must be understood in terms of our collective history. Both proclaim the reality of salvation in the here and now of social existence. In order to truly understand the significance of Jesus and the Christian community Gutiérrez feels that we must first "secularlize" our understanding of history. We must realize that we are responsible for its shape. Once this awareness takes root, our understanding of Jesus and self-understanding as Christians assume new dimensions. We begin to see ourselves as co-creators of history rather than passive observers. Gutiérrez describes the dynamics of the secularization process as follows:

> From a cosmological vision, man moves to an anthropological vision. . . . Man perceives himself as a creative subject. Moreover, man

becomes aware — as we have noted above — that he is an agent of history, responsible for his own destiny. His mind discovers not only the laws of nature, but also penetrates those of society, history, and psychology. This new self-understanding of man necessarily brings in its wake a different way of conceiving his relationship with God.[5]

A synonym Gutiérrez uses to describe this process is "worldliness." Borrowed from Bonhoeffer, the concept implies leaving behind ideological explanations of history and society and consciously assuming responsibility within it. For Gutiérrez worldliness "is a must, a necessary condition for an authentic relationship between man and nature, of men among themselves, and finally, between man and God."[6]

Jesus and Liberative Praxis

Gutiérrez has spent most of his life working for the liberation of the poor. Few people can equal his grasp of the complexity and difficulties of this process. Fewer still can match his faith in its inevitable triumph. Such faith might seem unjustified in a country like Peru where oppression and violence are the stuff of daily life, but these sinful realities are simply not the final word for Gutiérrez. The final word belongs to Jesus, who, by virtue of his message of God's reign and resurrection, shows us a way out of the impasse of oppression. For Gutiérrez Jesus gives coherence to the historical struggle of the poor for full humanity. He is the unsurpassable paradigm and symbol of liberation who "gives full meaning to filiation, which in its turn is the basis for human fellowship."[7] Jesus reveals what it means to be fully human and by doing so helps us glimpse the mysterious reality of God.

Although Gutiérrez's christology is not as systematically elaborated as that of other Latin American theologians such as Jon Sobrino or Juan Luis Segundo, it is nonetheless well developed. Using Pauline theology and the "high" christology characteristic of that tradition, Gutiérrez views Jesus as *the* central person in history who gives it a unique coherence and finality — ultimate assimilation into the reign of God. Thus,

the work of Christ is a new creation. In this sense, Paul speaks of a "new creation" in Christ (Gal. 6:15; 2 Cor. 5:17). Moreover, it is through this "new creation," that is to say, though the salvation which Christ affords, that creation acquires its full meaning (cf. Rom. 8).[8]

The centrality of Jesus is stressed even more directly in *A Theology of Liberation,* where he writes that "there is only one history — a 'Christo-finalized' history,"[9] thus asserting that every facet of life, including our historical and social existence, finds its ultimate point of reference in Jesus, who is God's invitation to participate in the salvation of our world.

Jesus sums up the inner meaning of history and challenges us to reshape
society in accord with his vision of God's reign. By accepting this call we
"see, hear, and touch"[10] Jesus like his first disciples.

Gutiérrez portrays Jesus as the incarnation of God's promise of salvation that "*is already* fulfilled in historical events, but *not yet* completely."
He is "the Promise [that] illuminates and fructifies the future of humanity
and leads it through incipient realizations towards its fullness."[11] Accordingly, Jesus' life and words give a new definition and inner logic to oppressed
peoples' search for liberation. He unites the struggles of the past, present,
and future by making them part of a contiguous salvific process in history.

> Jesus has already come into the world; this is true. He is a historical
> fact. But far from closing history, this fact opens it to unsuspected
> thoroughfares. Christ is not only come, he is the one who is to come.
> He is the future of our history.[12]

Jesus embodies the "future of history" in the sense that his preaching,
particularly that related to the reign of God, "reveals to society itself the
aspiration for a just society and leads it to discover unsuspected dimensions
and unexplored paths."[13] He pulls us out of our narrow, ideology-bound
worlds and provides us with a more sweeping vision of history and what it
means to be human.

Gutiérrez sees a correlation between Jesus' message of God's approaching reign and the utopian hopes of people throughout history. He views
them as related in the sense that both "postulate the unceasing search for a
new kind of man in a qualitatively different society,"[14] but ultimately distinct to the extent that "there is close relationship but no identification."[15]
This is a key methodological point since Gutiérrez refuses to absolutize
any utopian vision or political action on its behalf. By stressing the distinction between our relative, sometimes flawed efforts on behalf of liberation and the absolute symbols of God's reign as preached by Jesus,
Gutiérrez avoids the pitfall of "idolatry toward unavoidably ambiguous human achievement"[16] as well as the trap of Pelagianism.[17]

Gutiérrez understands Jesus' preaching of the reign of God as a call
to integral liberation or "*salvation* [that] *embraces the whole man.*"[18] This
necessarily involves a struggle against anything that impedes full human
development and the creation of a just society.

> Christ thus appears as the Savior who, by liberating us from sin,
> liberates us from the very root of social injustice. The entire dy-
> namism of human history, the struggle against all that depersonalizes
> man — social inequalities, misery, exploitation — have their origin, are
> sublimated, and reach their plenitude in the salvific work of Christ.[19]

Accordingly, Gutiérrez, quoting Pannenberg, considers the reign of God
to be politically subversive "in the very nucleus of its message" since it

calls for "the end of domination of man over man; it is a Kingdom of contradiction to the established powers and on behalf of man."[20] This explains why Jesus condemned the socio-religious establishment of his day. He saw it as contrary to God's historical plan for humanity, an impediment to salvation, and manifestation of sin.

The society he lived in was constructed on the basis of rigid class distinctions. An elite in Jerusalem considered itself inherently superior to ordinary people, not only socially but morally. What was far worse, however, was that they used a distorted, ideological definition of God to justify their oppressive righteousness. For Jesus this is the ultimate sin since it turns God into the venal self-image of the ruling class. The reign of God he preaches condemns such idolatry. It is a radical critique of all hierarchy as an affront to God's gratuitous love offered to all without distinction. Jesus preaches a message of crisis and judgment that condemns the presuppositions that hold together an oppressive state and religious system. Naturally the reaction to his words on the part of the privileged is violent.

Gutiérrez's understanding of Jesus displays characteristics of both a "high" and "low" christology. Jesus is the unsurpassable symbol of the incarnation, yet the message he preaches necessarily involves him in the socioreligious struggles of his day. For Gutiérrez these are correlative rather than contradictory qualities. In almost creedal language he describes Jesus as a person who "loved the poor by preference and for them confronted the great and powerful of his times, and he was put to death as subversive: he is God." At the same time "Jesus is the intrusion into history of the Son in whom all things were made and in whom all things were saved."[21] In accord with orthodox formulations, he both affirms Jesus' transcendence as the son of God and his total humanity. Jesus unites the divine and human thus setting a dynamic process of communication in motion that moves

> ...from people to God and from God to people; from history to faith and from faith to history; from the human word to the word of the Lord and from the word of the Lord to the human word; from fraternal love to the love of the Father and from the love of the Father to fraternal love; from human justice to the holiness of God and from the holiness of God to human justice; from poor to God and God to poor.[22]

In short, Gutiérrez perceives Jesus as "the principal hermeneutic of the faith"[23] who explains God's salvific presence in history and simultaneously asks us to respond to it in our particular social context. As Schillebeeckx points out, Gutiérrez's portrait of Jesus, along with that of other liberation theologians, avoids "the inauthentic dilemma of a decision between God and man"[24] because Jesus' humanity once and for all demonstrates God's presence among us.

Taking his lead from Dietrich Bonhoeffer, Gutiérrez feels that Jesus' life must be viewed as a continuum that moves from incarnation, to crucifixion, to resurrection.[25] When we examine the first two steps in this process — without which the last in impossible — the fact that Jesus, far from being either majestic or powerful, is born in poverty and oppression and executed as a political criminal assumes a crucial hermeneutic importance. For Bonhoeffer and Gutiérrez Jesus speaks of a God who is incomprehensible in an ideological, hierarchical society. The God he preaches has nothing to do with the trappings of power. This is a God who demands integrity and truthfulness, virtues that power brokers consider weaknesses. Gutiérrez summarizes the notion of the "weakness" of God as follows:

> God is a God who saves us not through his domination but through his suffering. Here we have Bonhoeffer's famous thesis of God's *weakness*. . . . It is of this God, and only of this God, that the Bible tells us. And it is thus that the cross acquires its tremendous revelatory potential with respect to God's weakness as an expression of his love for a world come of age.[26]

Gutiérrez insists that we grasp both the realism and necessity of Jesus' crucifixion. He is an intolerable threat to those in power, a dangerous iconoclast who refuses to worship the powers and principalities of his day. At first sight the cross seems to represent defeat rather than victory since Jesus dies a weak and beaten human being whose last words speak of despair. And yet this person who apparently has been silenced is raised from the dead. Rather than being conquered, the hope that Jesus proclaimed in his announcement of the reign of God continues on in his spirit. His resurrection condemns the sinfulness and lack of vision of his oppressors.

The so-called weakness of God evident in Jesus' life is used by Gutiérrez as a hermeneutic key that unlocks the deeper significance of oppressed peoples' suffering. Like Jesus the poor are victimized, but their poverty and pain are not the last word. To the extent that they struggle to make justice and equality real in their own lives and society their suffering assumes a different meaning. As Gutiérrez points out in *The Power of the Poor in History,* their constant efforts to achieve liberation in history are not wasted energy but a cumulative effort whose ultimate triumph is foreshadowed in Jesus' resurrection.

> The key to every theological interpretation is Christ, and it was precisely the coherence of Christ's word with his practice that led him to his death. A christological approach makes it possible to subsume the experiences of, and reflections on, the faith that the poor have realized throughout the course of history, and incorporate these experiences and reflections into a valid and authentic theology. At the same time a christological perspective will open for us the future of the resurrection — the life that conquers death, and that we know we

have within us "because we love our brothers and sisters" (cf. 1 John 3:14).[27]

As Gutiérrez makes clear, the struggle to break down the social barriers that separate people and social classes is part of an effort to undo the effects of sin. It is a manifestation of love that strives to make human solidarity and justice real facets of life despite distorted and destructive definitions of its purpose. Jesus stands as proof that the hope evident in these acts of love in society is not in vain. Although it may be momentarily stymied, such hope contributes bit by bit to the process of liberation whose ultimate victory is a fundamental precept of Christian faith.

The Christian Community and Liberative Praxis

Gutiérrez believes that Jesus' life and resurrection continue on in history. His struggle to overcome the effects of sin and lay the groundwork for the reign of God are "dangerous memories"[28] that continue to challenge our consciences. The provocative memory of Jesus lives on in the church, that community of people who believe that the same God who raised Jesus lives in their midst. Quoting Teilhard de Chardin, Gutiérrez refers to the church as "the reflexively 'Christified' part of humanity" which is moving toward "the future promised by the Lord."[29]

Logically, then, any "understanding of the church begins with christology"[30] to the extent that Jesus' life is its paradigm and support. The church is charged with keeping alive his "dangerous memory" and making that memory a real social force. In societies weighed down by oppression the Christian community clearly plays a subversive role: it denounces the affliction of the poor and announces God's call to liberation. For Gutiérrez the church is a "sacrament of history."[31] It is a sign of God's saving presence in the struggle for full humanity and celebrates the small but significant steps the oppressed take toward liberation.

As an expression of Jesus' spirit the Christian community makes itself vulnerable as he was. It is subject to ridicule and persecution because it rejects the false absolutes and oppressive beliefs of socio-religious elites as he did in his own historical context.

> An ecclesiology whose point of departure is Christ calling us out from the midst of the oppressed can furnish us with the guidelines we need to locate the church in today's concrete situation in Latin America. Today, worsening hunger and exploitation, as well as exile and imprisonment...torture and death...make up the price to be paid for having rebelled against a secular oppression. They are the price to be paid for having begun to understand what it is to be Christian, and to be church, in our day.[32]

The church Gutiérrez speaks of, like Jesus, also embodies God's "weakness." This is a church of the powerless and, for this reason, an enigma in an oppressive society. It assumes the perspective and experience of the poor as its norms, not those of the powerful. What power it "has" is not its own but rather a trust. Its power is the "counter-power" of God's demand for justice as announced by Jesus. It is a guardian of a power oppressors cannot understand. For Gutiérrez the only authentic church is one that is truly of and for the people or, in more descriptive Spanish, *una iglesia popular*. This church, or Christian community, remembers its members' pain, gives courage, and celebrates their hope of liberation.

Given the history of Christianity in Latin America, the church Gutiérrez describes is radically innovative. The Catholic Church is a recognized power throughout the continent, but its power has all too often accrued from a symbiotic relationship with the ruling elite. In exchange for recognition and prestige the institutional church has often blunted the cutting message of God's reign as Jesus preached it. For Gutiérrez the most effective way to counteract this unfortunate legacy is to "reappropriate" the gospel. The demanding vision of God's reign must be foremost in the church's mind. It must become an "anti-ideological" community compelled by the gospel to struggle against the false values and systemic oppression of the status quo as Jesus himself did.

If this struggle is to be effective it must be well thought out and organized. Gutiérrez recognizes the legitimacy of the church as structured institution. He knows full well that the Christian community needs order like any social body. But its institutional structure must serve the oppressed rather than the oppressors. Fortunately the church in Latin America has begun to do just that. Gutiérrez was closely involved in the preparations for the episcopal conferences of Medellín and Puebla. He has been a close advisor and friend of many Peruvian bishops. In the last twenty years he has seen members of the Catholic hierarchy act with prophetic courage. Men who once acted like feudal lords have opted to be one with the poor at the price of condemnation as "Marxists" and even death.

As the Christian communities of Latin America reappropriate the gospel, they redefine what it means to be church. What was previously a staid, hierarchical institution is becoming a community of brothers and sisters. Gutiérrez describes the dynamics of this process of ecclesial transformation:

> We are talking about the creation of Christian communities in which the private owners of the goods of this world cease to be the owners of the gospel. "Rebellious communities" they were called premonitiously years ago. Communities, we would add today, in which the dispossessed can realize a social reappropriation of the Gospel, groups which announce prophetically a church entirely at the service, always creative and critical, of persons who fight to be persons.[33]

This newly "creative and critical" church reflects the human characteristics of its members. Their history, language, and culture are important parts of its "tradition." As Gutiérrez mentions in blunt terms, when the church is truly an expression of the oppressed peoples' lives and faith, "to preach the gospel will be a rock of scandal, it will be a gospel 'unpresentable in society.' It will be expressed in an unrefined manner, it will smell bad."[34] It will smell of the aspirations of the poor for dignity and equality that oppressors find difficult to tolerate.

It is important to realize that although the Christian community "reappropriates" the gospel it does not turn it into a possession. For Gutiérrez the gospel has a "permanently creative and critical nature."[35] As such it can never be totally understood nor assimilated by any ecclesial structure, be it institutional Catholicism or the local base community. The gospel is primary, the church secondary. Revising this equation leads to tragic consequences. The gospel's cutting edge is blunted as it is tamed and "socialized" while the church loses an indispensable criterion for judging its own actions.

As the history of Catholicism in Latin America amply demonstrates, a church that tries to possess the gospel ends up using it perversely. The challenge is to assess constantly the Christian community's commitment to the gospel by juxtaposing its all too fallible actions with the vision of Jesus. In this way the Christian community avoids the danger of falling victim to what Gutiérrez calls "ecclesiocentrism,"[36] a tendency to look self-assuredly within itself as if it were somehow the privileged repository of God's word. In its worst form "ecclesiocentrism" produces an institutional narcissism that confuses the gospel with the relative structures of the church.

It is equally important to note that Gutiérrez does not see the church, even the church of the poor, as a salvific institution. He insists that God alone saves. Nonetheless, the church plays a part in the salvific process to the extent that it is an expression of Jesus' life. He spells this out clearly in one of his earliest works:

What then is the mission of the Church? We will respond unequivocally that its mission is not to save in the sense that only within it does one find salvation. The one who saves is Christ. However, the Church certainly has a salvific mission, which consists in revealing the active presence of salvation among men — communion with God. The Church can reveal to men the presence of salvation effected by Christ in virtue of being the depository of God's word. The word of God has the power of revealing the enigma of history, of unraveling the mystery of salvation; . . . basically the church reveals its experience of communion with God and with men.[37]

The church is called on to be a sign of God's coming reign despite its obvious limitations and occasional infidelity. In societies as oppressive as those of Latin America, the Christian community thus provides an indispensable service to society at large. By its fidelity to the gospel it keeps alive an alternative model of what it means to be a human being in societies where violence and dehumanization are the order of the day.

In his varied analyses of the church Gutiérrez has worked out a very nuanced explanation of Christian social action that deserves close scrutiny. It is far more sophisticated than that of any other liberation theologian and totally unrelated to the simplistic characterization evident in the first Vatican instruction on liberation theology.[38] For Gutiérrez Christians become politically involved because they have a responsibility to history. If their faith does not prod them to struggle for their oppressed sisters and brothers their faith is a useless abstraction. But it is crucially important not to confuse that political action with the reign of God itself, which, as Gutiérrez has always pointed out, "is a gift of the Lord."[39]

The reign of God stands above us. It judges our political action. To lose sight of this fact or equate political action with God's will is to make a mistake of tragic proportions. We must keep in mind the relativity of politics and the absoluteness of God's coming reign. If this distinction is kept in mind we can avoid the dangers of either "politico-religious messianism" or a "two-kingdom" type of split between political action and faith. Given the importance and delicacy of this topic we quote Gutiérrez at length:

> To assert that there is a direct, immediate relationship between faith and political action encourages one to seek from faith norms and criteria for particular political options. To be really effective these options ought to be based on rational analyses of reality. Thus confusions are created which can result in a dangerous politico-religious messianism which does not sufficiently respect either the autonomy of the political arena or that which belongs to an authentic faith. . . .
>
> On the other hand, to assert that faith and political action have nothing to say to each other is to imply that they move on juxtaposed and unrelated planes. If one accepts this assertion, either he will have to engage in verbal gymnastics to show — without succeeding — how faith should express itself in a commitment to a more just society; or the result is that faith comes to coexist, in a more opportunistic manner, with any political option.[40]

As the central symbol of Christian faith the reign of God points to the inherent inadequacy of "all historical instances of liberation."[41] At the same time it compels the Christian to engage in political action aimed at overcoming oppression that denies that we are created "in the image and likeness of God" (Gn. 1:26–27).

As a body of believers that both denounces and announces God's coming reign, the Christian community does not make what Latin Americans call a "party option," although this is not true of the individual Christian.

It cannot link itself with any given political organization, be it that which resists the status quo or that which supports it. To do so would be to confuse the relative with the absolute and jeopardize the church's credibility as a symbol of God's coming reign. At the same time the Christian community cannot be politically neutral, for that would be to act irresponsibly. If it countenances oppression, it contradicts its evangelical purpose. Thus the church, in a manner of speaking, is "above" but not "out" of politics. In Hegelian terms, it is in dialectical tension with the political sphere.

As Gutiérrez sees it the church's primary role is to act as an ethical guide. As such it points out a society's failings and calls for redoubled efforts to create a more liberated world in accord with the plan of creation. He calls this on-going process the "prophetic mission" of the Christian community.

> For this reason we say that the church has a prophetic mission that includes the formulation of judgment. The word of God allows the Church to reveal the mystery of history and judge it. Judgment is an important evangelical theme. Judgment is that which, in a certain way, effects union between human reality and the word of God in order to give human history the direction which the word of God desires. Judgment allows the word of God to become incarnate, to make itself history, and, at the same time, to divinize history. In accord with its prophetic mission the church must denounce that which is opposed to man and places an obstacle between human communion and communion with God.[42]

As we saw previously, denunciation or judgment is always followed by annunciation. The annunciation of the Christian community is that "the love of the Father calls all men in Christ and through the action of the Spirit to union among themselves and communion with him."[43]

Effective denunciation and annunciation require a clear and critical socio-historical sense. The members of the Christian community must have an informed understanding of themselves and their role in society. They must know why they are poor and find ways of overcoming their oppression. Their denunciation of oppression will have an impact only if it intelligently challenges the social forces and agents that cause it. Likewise, the annunciation of their hope will be effective only if it leads to real socio-political change. If this is not the case the church of the poor runs the risk of becoming a sect whose unreal pronouncements and expectations will have no liberating effect. This, of course, is the last thing Gutiérrez wants. He sees the popular church as an integrated and well informed social body with solid criteria of action that it arrives at through a continual process of analysis, reflection, and, he insists with great frequency, prayer.

For Gutiérrez the political activity of the Christian community flows naturally from what it means to be church in an oppressive society. It is a response to the challenge of ethical social behavior set forth in Matthew 25:31–46. Thus,

> ... what we do for the poor we do to Christ himself. It is this fact that gives action in behalf of the poor its decisive character and prevents it from being taken simply as an expression of the "social dimension" of faith. No, it is much more than that; such action has an element of contemplation, of encounter with God, at the very heart of the work of love.[44]

In Latin America a church whose purpose is "the work of love" has no choice but to confront the continent's preeminent evil — class stratification. Gutiérrez states that the principal "function of the ecclesial community is to struggle against the profound causes of the division among men." The church is called to be "an effective sign of unity."[45] Its inner cohesion and the joy of a shared vision counteract the competition and fragmentation characteristic of capitalist society.

The church of the poor Gutiérrez advocated in the late 1960s has become a reality in the *comunidades de base* now so widespread in Latin America. During the last two decades his commitment to this utopic, socially involved form of church has grown in tandem with his knowledge of its working dynamics. Grassroots experience has taught him that basic Christian communities are the most effective way to vitalize the life of the institutional church in his country and continent. It has also taught him that if Christians struggle for liberation they can expect a violent reaction from power brokers. As he points out in one of his latest works, suspicion of the popular church "is nowadays a component of the cross of Christians who seek to bear witness to the Gospel of the poor."[46]

This suspicion involves more than skepticism and disagreement. It has generated persecution that in some cases has been abetted by certain members of the ecclesiastical hierarchy. As Gutiérrez points out in poignant terms, the church of the poor is passing through a period of martyrdom:

> There are many who have devoted their lives, to the point of suffering death, in order to bear witness to the presence of the poor in the Latin American world and to the preferential love that God has for them. Nor has the bloodletting ceased as yet. The first manifestations of this unparalleled and astonishing situation (after all, when many of the persecutors and murderers come out into the open they claim to be Christians) go back to about 1968. We are perhaps still too close historically to these events to be able to gauge their full significance.[47]

Yet, rather than diminishing Christians' resolve, persecution has increased it. It has helped them better understand their role in society as people who bear a message of hope despite the ravages of oppression. Their maturity as people of faith has grown as the price of commitment has risen.

We are not now in the evening of the history of the church but are beginning the new day of an opportunity for evangelization that we never had before.

To some this may smack of facile and naïve optimism. True enough, the exhaustion produced by an unending situation of wretchedness; the tension caused by the resistance men and women must engage in if they are to win out in their commitment to liberation; the depression felt as the abiding attitude of suspicion that greets every effort at effective solidarity with an exploited people; the resistance experienced within the people of God itself — these facts do not permit an easy optimism or allow us to forget the marginalization, the suffering, the deaths. At the same time, however, we must be aware of the change that has taken place. When all is said and done, despite — or thanks to — the immense price that is being paid, the present situation is nourishing new life, revealing new paths to be followed, and providing reason for profound joy.[48]

What Gutiérrez describes is a church of the poor trying to be faithful to its vision of Jesus. It is a group of men and women struggling to overcome sin in their societies and open them up to the reign of God. Their success has been notable despite furious and bloody persecution.

The church in Latin America enjoys a credibility it has never had before because it has become a sign of real evangelical orthopraxis. As Gutiérrez mentions, this does not mean that the community of believers is immune from internal problems. It is not an infallible institution but a community trying to respond to the challenge of liberative praxis as best it can. There is no single analytical approach, no one theological system or spirituality in the struggle for integral liberation, and so debate among Christians is inevitable. For Gutiérrez, however, this plurality is not a problem but a sign of life.

When Gutiérrez is not in Rimac he is apt to be in other parts of Peru or Latin America helping to strengthen the local church. He shares his faith and theological insights as a brother with a vision and commitment to the poor. As he sees it, his theology is not so much his own as the fruit of his fellow Christians' experience and thought. He sees himself as their spokesperson and his theology as a reflection of their Spirit-given wisdom. He is a man devoid of pretense or possessiveness who realizes that the gifts he has are the property of the Christian community.

Gutiérrez has helped reshape and revitalize the church of Peru and Latin America in ways that are still difficult to calculate. What was once a hierarchical institution far removed from the lives of ordinary people is now opting for the poor. The church is becoming a community of believers, an embodiment of the faith of an oppressed but believing people. It is increasingly prophetic and life-giving. This radical transformation owes much to Gutiérrez. He has shaken the consciences of bishops who have come to see him as an ally and friend and shared his vision of hope with *campesinos* who relate to him as a brother. His writings and presence among the poor have helped create truly ecclesial communities that put the lie to oppression and prove that the final and most powerful word is God's love.

In many ways Gutiérrez's theology has a single purpose — to give vitality and purpose to Christians committed to the the cause of liberation. Their progress is slow and painful, but nonetheless real. By way of conclusion I cite a passage from the Colombian novelist García Márquez found in *We Drink from Our Own Wells*. It speaks beautifully of the faith and hope of the oppressed. It also splendidly sums up who Gustavo Gutiérrez is and what his theology is about — hope.

> Faced with oppression, pillage, and abandonment, our response is life.... It is a new and splendid utopia of life, where no one can decide for others how they will die, where love will be certain and happiness possible, and where those condemned to a hundred years of solitary confinement find, finally and forever, a second chance on this earth.[49]

NOTES

1. Frank E. Manuel and Fritzie P. Manuel, *Utopian Thought in the Western World* (Cambridge, Mass.: Belknap Press of Harvard University Press, 1979), p. 28.
2. Gutiérrez, *A Theology of Liberation: History, Politics, and Salvation*, trans. and ed. Sister Caridad Inda and John Eagleson (Maryknoll, N.Y.: Orbis books, 1973), p. 13.
3. Ibid., p. 6. In this part of the book Gutiérrez spells out his understanding of theology. Although short, this first chapter is important methodologically and sets the tone for the whole work.
4. Ibid., p. 194.
5. Ibid., p. 67.
6. Ibid.
7. Gutiérrez, *We Drink from Our Own Wells: The Spiritual Journey of a People* (Maryknoll, N.Y.: Orbis Books, and Melbourne, Dove Communications, 1984), p. 38.
8. Gutiérrez, *A Theology of Liberation*, p. 158.
9. Ibid., p. 153.
10. Gutiérrez, *We Drink from Our Own Wells*, p. 38.
11. Gutiérrez, *A Theology of Liberation*, p. 161.
12. Gutiérrez, *The Power of the Poor in History: Selected Writings*, trans. Robert R. Barr (Maryknoll, N.Y.: Orbis Books, 1983), p. 13.
13. Gutiérrez, *A Theology of Liberation*, pp. 231–232.
14. Ibid., p. 231.
15. Ibid., p. 171.
16. Ibid., p. 238.
17. In the first Vatican instruction on liberation theology the statement is made that certain theologians "have substituted a figure of Jesus who is a kind of symbol who

sums up in himself the requirements of the struggle of the oppressed" for the authentic Jesus of Catholic tradition. If the accusation is being made of Gutiérrez's christology it is unfounded. See "Instruction on Certain Aspects of the 'Theology of Liberation' from the Congregation for the Doctrine of the Faith," *Origins* 14 (September 13, 1984), p. 202, paragraph 11.

18. Gutiérrez, "Notes for a Theology of Liberation," *Theological Studies* 31 (1970): 256.
19. Ibid., p. 257.
20. Gutiérrez, *A Theology of Liberation*, p. 231.
21. Gutiérrez and Shaull, *Liberation and Change*, ed. Ronald H. Stone (Atlanta: John Knox Press, 1977), p. 83.
22. Ibid.
23. Ibid.
24. Schillebeeckx, *Christ: The Experience of Jesus as Lord*, trans. John Bowden (New York: Crossroad, 1981), p. 761.
25. See Gutiérrez, *The Power of the Poor*, p. 227.
26. Ibid., p. 230.
27. Ibid., pp. 104–105.
28. The concept of Jesus as a "dangerous memory" comes from the writings of the German political theologian Johann Baptist Metz. Gutiérrez is quite familiar with Metz's theology. His analysis of the subversive undercurrent in history in many ways parallels Metz's thought. See Johann Baptist Metz, *Faith in History and Society: Toward a Practical Fundamental Theology* (New York: Seabury, 1980), especially pp. 88–99.
29. Gutiérrez, *Theological Studies* 31: 259.
30. Gutiérrez, *The Power of the Poor*, p. 210.
31. Gutiérrez, *A Theology of Liberation*, p. 268. Chapter 12 of this work is a treatise on ecclesiology unmatched in its sophistication and challenge.
32. Gutiérrez, *The Power of the Poor*, p. 211.
33. Gutiérrez, *Praxis of Liberation and Christian Faith: Notes on a Course Given at M.A.C.C.*, (San Antonio: Mexican American Cultural Center, 1974), p. 56.
34. Gutiérrez and Shaull, p. 93.
35. Gutiérrez, "Liberation, Theology and Proclamation," in *Concilium* 96, *The Mystical and Political Dimension of the Christian Faith*, ed. Claude Geffré and Gustavo Gutiérrez (New York: Herder and Herder, 1974), p. 74.
36. Gutiérrez, *The Power of the Poor*, p. 210.
37. Gutiérrez, *Líneas pastorales de la Iglesia en América Latina: un análisis teológico* (Lima: Centro de Estudios y Publicaciones, 1970), p. 69.
38. The document in question states that "there is a tendency to identify the kingdom of God and its growth with the human liberation movement and to make history itself the subject of its own development." Just how erroneous this opinion is should be immediately clear. See "Instruction on Certain Aspects of the 'Theology of Liberation,'" p. 210, paragraph 3.
39. Gutiérrez, Liberation Movements and Theology," in *Concilium* 93, *Jesus Christ and Human Freedom*, ed. Edward Schillebeeckx and Bas van Iersel (New York: Herder and Herder, 1974), p. 144.
40. Gutiérrez, *A Theology of Liberation*, p. 236.
41. Gutiérrez, *Concilium* 93: p. 144.
42. Gutiérrez, *Líneas pastorales de la Iglesia en América Latina*, p. 70.
43. Gutiérrez, *A Theology of Liberation*, p. 268.
44. Gutiérrez, *We Drink from Our Own Wells*, p. 104.
45. Gutiérrez, *A Theology of Liberation*, p. 278.
46. Gutiérrez, *We Drink from Our Own Wells*, pp. 12–13.
47. Ibid., pp. 22–23.
48. Ibid., pp. 24–25.
49. Gutiérrez, *We Drink from Our Own Wells*, p. 27.

Bibliography

Works by Gutiérrez

The list below contains nearly all of Gutiérrez's writings since 1970. Wherever it seemed useful I have added comments. Gutiérrez tends to rewrite and republish articles using slightly altered titles. Many of the articles he wrote in the mid-1970s were reissued in *The Power of the Poor in History*. That text along with *A Theology of Liberation* and *We Drink from Our Own Wells* represent the bulk of his writings to date. His latest work, *Hablar de Dios* has been published in English as *On Job: God-Talk and the Suffering of the Innocent*. In mid-1986 he published *La verdad los hará libres*, which contains key essays published in *Páginas* as well as new material which attempts to set forth his theological method and respond to its critics.

Gutiérrez, Gustavo. *Líneas pastorales de la iglesia en América Latina: un análisis teológico*. Lima: Centro de Estudios y Publicaciones, 1970, 91 pages. An early treatise on ecclesiology. Its main ideas can be found in *A Theology of Liberation*.

————. "Notes for a Theology of Liberation." *Theological Studies* 31 (1970): 243–261. This article is essentially a synopsis of *A Theology of Liberation*.

————. "Cristianos latinoamericanos y socialismo." Bogotá: *CEDIAL* 29 (1972): 15–34. In this essay Gutiérrez discusses the relationship between Christianity and socialism.

————. *Teología de la liberación: perspectivas*. Lima: Centro de Estudios y Publicaciones, 1971, 384 pages; Salamanca: Sígueme, 1972, 399 pages. Published in English as *A Theology of Liberation: History, Politics, and Salvation*. Translated and edited by Sister Caridad Inda and John Eagleson. Maryknoll, N.Y.: Orbis Books, 1973, 323 pages. This book is the most important work by Gutiérrez. Despite its publication date, it remains his most thorough and challenging work.

————. "Liberation Movements and Theology." In *Concilium* 93, *Jesus Christ and Human Freedom*. Ed. Edward Schillebeeckx and Bas van Iersel. New York: Herder and Herder, 1974, pp. 135–146.

————. "Praxis de liberación, teología y evangelización," in *Liberación: diálogos en el CELAM*. Bogotá: CELAM, 1974, pp. 68–85.

Bibliography

————. "Liberation, Theology and Proclamation." In *Concilium* 96, *The Mystical and Political Dimension of the Christian Faith.* Ed. Claude Geffré and Gustavo Gutiérrez. New York: Herder and Herder, 1974, pp. 55–77.

————. *Praxis of Liberation and Christian Faith: Notes on a Course Given at M.A.C.C.* San Antonio: Mexican American Cultural Center, 1974, 63 pages. This is a slightly altered and condensed version of *A Theology of Liberation.*

————. "Jesús y el mundo político." In *Panorama de la teología latinoamericana* I. Salamanca: Sígueme, 1975, pp. 105–115. This work considers the relationship between Jesus' preaching and the political realm.

————. "Créativité chrétienne: Pour une théologie et une liturgie de la libération." *Bulletin de Liaison International* (Nantes, 1976): 5 pages.

————. "Statement by Gustavo Gutiérrez." In *Theology in the Americas.* Ed. Sergio Torres and John Eagleson. Maryknoll, N.Y.: Orbis Books, 1976, pp. 309–313.

————. "Revelación y anuncio de Dios en la historia." *Páginas* Separata 2:1 (1976): pp. 1–12. This article, also published in Bogotá in *Pastoral Popular* 27, no. 145 (1976), speaks of revelation and God's place in history.

————. "Bartolomé de Las Casas: Libertad y liberación." *Páginas* 5–6 (1976): pp. 41–49. Gutiérrez analyzes the theology of Bartolomé de Las Casas, a sixteenth-century Dominican who championed the cause of oppressed indigenous peoples in Latin America.

————, and Richard Shaull. "Freedom and Salvation: A Political Problem." In *Liberation and Change.* Atlanta: John Knox Press, 1977, 200 pages. This short work contains an analysis of the Enlightenment and principles behind capitalism.

————. "The Poor in the Church." In *Concilium* 104, *The Poor and the Church.* Ed. Norbert Greinacher and Alöis Müller. New York: Seabury Press, 1977, pp. 11–16.

————. "Sobre el documento de consulta para Puebla." *Misiones Extranjeras* 45 (1978): pp. 168–198. This work, published in Madrid, reflects on the draft agenda statement of the approaching Puebla meeting. It is an important document in terms of Gutiérrez's ecclesial posture and reading of the tensions within the Latin America church at the time.

————. "Two Theological Perspectives: Liberation Theology and Progressive Theology." In *The Emergent Gospel.* Ed. Sergio Torres and Virginia Fabella, M.M. Maryknoll, N.Y.: Orbis Books, 1978, pp. 227–255.

————. "¿Evangelizar la cultura, evasión de un compromiso?: Análisis crítico del Documento de consulta." *Servir* 14, no. 75 (1978): pp. 399–442. As the title indicates, this article, published in *Servir*, a Mexican journal, criticizes the theological position of the first agenda proposal for the Puebla Conference.

————. "Por fuera de la asamblea." *Theologica Xaveriana* 29: 1, no. 50 (1979): pp. 55–87. A series of interviews "outside of the assembly" with noted liberation theologians who were excluded from the Puebla meeting. Gutiérrez, Boff, Segundo, and others provide their insights on the conference.

————. "Los límites de la teología moderna: Un texto de Bonhoeffer." In *Concilium* 145 (Spanish edition), Madrid (1979): pp. 222–236. An analysis of Bonhoeffer's theology as distinguished from the ideas of Barth, Tillich, and Bultmann.

———. "Liberation Praxis and Christian Faith." In *Frontiers of Theology in Latin America*. Ed. Rosino Gibellini. Maryknoll, N.Y.: Orbis Books, 1979, pp. 1–33.

———. "Oro y evangelio: El anónimo de Yucay." *Páginas* 4 Separata 20 (1979): pp. 1–11. This article was rewritten and reissued in 1981 as "El Dios de la Vida." It considers the history of evangelization, theology, and the poor in colonial Peru.

———. *Los pobres y la liberación en Puebla*. Bogotá: Indo-American Press, 1979. As the title indicates, this article deals with the Puebla Conference and its posture towards the poor.

———. "Comunidades cristianas de base: perspectivas eclesiológicas," *Páginas* 5 (1980): pp. 3–13. In this article Gutiérrez asserts that the church must arise from the experience of the poor.

———. "La violencia de un sistema." In *Concilium* 160 (Spanish edition), Madrid, 1980, pp. 565–575. In this article Gutiérrez speaks of the contradictory values of capitalism and the need for a new ethical system based on believing communities of people.

———. "Un pueblo oprimido y creyente, y las comunidades cristianas de base." *Puebla* 15 (1981), pp. 926–933. Gutiérrez describes the struggle of the poor for liberation as an integral part of evangelization.

———. "En busca de los pobres de Jesucristo: evangelización y teología en el siglo XVI." In *Materiales para una historia de la teología en América Latina: VIII Encuentro Latinoamericano de CEHILA, Lima*. Ed. Pablo Richard. San José, Costa Rica: DEI., 1981, pp. 137–163. This article considers the relationship among the poor, the concept of evangelization, and theology at the time of the Spanish Conquest.

———. "En busca de los pobres de Jesucristo." *Páginas* Separata 38 (June 1981) pp. 1–12. This article is a reworking of the reference above.

———. "Entre las calandrias." In *Arguedas: mito, historia y religión*. Lima: Centro de Estudios y Publicaciones, 1982, pp. 239–277. This monograph contains an analysis of Arguedas's writings.

———. "El evangelio del trabajo." In *Sobre el trabajo humano: Comentarios a la Encíclica "Laborem exercens."* Lima: Centro de Estudios y Publicaciones, 1982, pp. 9–64. Gutiérrez published this work soon after *Laborem Exercens* was issued. It is a crucial document since it shows the continuity between papal teaching and his theology.

———. "El Dios de la vida." *Páginas* 6 Separata 40 (1981): pp. 1–20. This article also appears in In *Cuadernos de Teología 1*, Lima: Pontificia Universidad Católica del Perú, 1982. It treats of the God of the Bible who is holy and alive as well as the idolatry of contemporary society that negates God's presence through oppression.

———. *La fuerza histórica de los pobres: selección de trabajos*. Lima: Centro de Estudios y Publicaciones, 1979, 423 pages. Published in English as *The Power of the Poor in History: Selected Writings*. Trans. Robert Barr. Maryknoll, N.Y.: Orbis Books, 1983, 240 pages. This anthology contains most of the essays Gutiérrez wrote during the 1970s and is crucial for understanding how his theological vision has evolved since the publication of *A Theology of Liberation*.

————. *Salvación y pobreza: Consecuencias eclesiológicas.* Lima: Pontificia Universidad Católica del Perú, XIII Jornada de Reflexión Teológica, 1983. Gutiérrez writes about salvation, poverty, and their meaning in ecclesial life.

————. "Reflections from a Latin American Perspective: Finding Our Way to Talk about God." In *Irruption of the Third World: Challenge to Theology.* Ed. Virginia Fabella, M.M., and Sergio Torres. Maryknoll, N.Y.: Orbis Books, 1983, pp. 222–234.

————. *Beber en su propio pozo: en el itinerario espiritual de un pueblo.* Lima: Centro de Estudios y Publicaciones, 1983. Published in English as *We Drink from Our Own Wells: The Spiritual Journey of a People.* Maryknoll, N.Y.: Orbis Books and Melbourne: Dove Communications, 1984, 181 pages. An extremely important book focusing on a spirituality for liberative praxis.

————. "The Task of Theology in Ecclesial Experience." In *Concilium* 176, *La Iglesia Popular: Between Fear and Hope.* Ed. Leonardo Boff and Virgil Elizondo. Edinburgh: T. & T. Clark, Ltd., 1984, pp. 61–64.

————. "Resurrección y evangelización de los gentiles." *Páginas* 11 (August 1984): pp. 2, 43.

————. "Teología y ciencias sociales." *Páginas* 11 (September 1984): pp. 4–15. Despite its brevity this article is an extremely important document. In it Gutiérrez analyses the relationship among the social sciences, Marxism, and theology. It was written in response to criticism from certain members of the hierarchy and attempts to address the issues set forth in the first Vatican document on liberation theology.

————. "Speaking about God." In *Concilium* 171, *Different Theologies, Common Responsibility: Babel or Pentecost.* Ed. Claude Geffré, Gustavo Gutiérrez, and Virgil Elizondo. Edinburgh: T. & T. Clark, Ltd., 1984, pp. 27–31.

————. "La visita del Papa vista por Gustavo Gutiérrez." *Quehacer* 33 (February 1985): pp. 17–25. An analysis of the papal trip to Peru made in 1985.

————. "Hambre de Dios: Si Hambre de Pan: No!" *La República* (February 6, 1985): pp. 3–4.

————. *Hablar de Dios desde el sufrimiento del inocente: Una reflexión sobre el libro de Job.* Lima: Instituto Bartolomé de las Casas and Centro de Estudios y Publicaciones, 1986, 226 pages. English translation: *On Job: God-Talk and the Suffering of the Innocent.* Trans. Matthew J. O'Connell. Maryknoll, N.Y.: Orbis Books, 1987, 156 pages. This work analyses Job's suffering and spirituality. It follows logically from *We Drink from Our Own Wells* in the sense that it is concerned with creating a deeper spirituality for liberative praxis.

————. "El Señor amigo de la vida." *Paz tarea de todos* 1 Separata 1 (October–November 1986): 4 pages. This article, published by C.E.A.S., the social action department of the Peruvian Episcopal Conference, is significant since in it Gutiérrez addresses the question of political violence in Peru.

————. *La verdad los hará libres: confrontaciones.* Lima: Centro de Estudios y Publicaciones, 1986, 250 pages. This work contains Gutiérrez's doctoral defense in Lyon, France, his crucial article on the relationship between the social sciences and theology, and a long essay on the content and implications of his theology.

Works about Gutiérrez and Interviews

Brockman, James R. "The Prophetic Role of the Church in Latin America: A Conversation with Gustavo Gutiérrez." *The Christian Century* 100 (October 19, 1983): pp. 931–935.

Brown, Robert McAfee. *Makers of Contemporary Theology: Gustavo Gutiérrez.* Atlanta: John Knox Press, 1980.

———. Preface to *The Power of the Poor in History* by Gustavo Gutiérrez. Maryknoll, N.Y.: Orbis Books, 1983.

———. "Espiritualidad y liberación: en favor de Gustavo Gutiérrez." *Páginas* Separata 65–66 (November–December 1984).

Chopp, Rebecca S. *The Praxis of Suffering: An Interpretation of Liberation and Political Theologies.* Maryknoll, N.Y.: Orbis Books, 1986.

Grández, Felix Moreno. "Entrevista a Gustavo Gutiérrez — La iglesia y el anuncio del evangelio en el momento actual." *Pastoral Andina* 54 (March–April 1986): 9–13.

Manzanera, Miguel. *Teología, salvación y liberación en la obra de Gustavo Gutiérrez.* Bilbao: Universidad de Deusto, 1978.

Peirano, Luis. "Entrevista con Gustavo Gutiérrez." *Quehacer* (March 1980): pp. 105–117.

Ramsey, William M. *Four Modern Prophets: Walter Rauschenbusch, Martin Luther King Jr., Gustavo Gutiérrez, Rosemary Radford Ruether.* Atlanta: John Knox Press, 1986.

Tamez, Elsa, ed. Interview with Gustavo Gutiérrez. In *Teólogos de la liberación hablan sobre la mujer.* San José, Costa Rica: DEI, 1986, pp. 51–59. Gutiérrez comments on the oppression of women and feminist theology. Published in English in *Against Machismo.* Ed. Elsa Tamez (Oak Park, Ill.: Meyer-Stone Books, 1987).

Works Cited

Althusser, Louis. "Ideology and Ideological State Apparatuses." In his *Lenin and Philosophy and Other Essays.* Trans. Ben Brewster. New York: Monthly Review Press, 1971.

Arguedas, José María. "La novela y el problema de la expresión literaria en el Perú." In *Yawar Fiesta.* Santiago: Editorial Universitaria, 1973.

———. *Deep Rivers.* Trans. Frances Horning Barraclough. Austin: University of Texas Press, 1978.

Baum, Gregory. *Religion and Alienation: A Theological Reading of Sociology.* New York: Paulist Press, 1975.

Bloch, Ernst. *Das Prinzip Hoffnung.* 2nd ed. Frankfurt: Suhrkamp, 1969.

Burns, Thomas. *Peru National Reality, 1984.* Mimeographed document prepared for the Maryknoll Fathers and Brothers, Peru Region.

Burns, Tomás. "...Y perdónanos nuestras deudas..." *Páginas* 9 (September 1984): pp. 24–33.

Cardoso, Fernando Henrique, and Enzo Faletto. *Dependency and Development in Latin America.* Trans. Marjory Mattingly Urquidi. Berkeley: University of California Press, 1979.

Comblin, José. *The Church and the National Security State*. Maryknoll, N.Y.: Orbis Books, 1979.
Coste, René. *Marxist Analysis and Christian Faith*. Maryknoll, N.Y.: Orbis Books, 1985.
Freire, Paulo. *Pedagogy of the Oppressed*. Translated by Myra Bergman Ramos. New York: Herder & Herder, 1970.
Geertz, Clifford. *The Interpretation of Cultures: Selected Essays by Clifford Geertz*. New York: Basic Books, 1973.
Girardi, Giulio. *Marxism and Christianity*. Trans. Kevin Traynor. New York: The Macmillan Company, 1968.
Gramsci, Antonio. *Selections from the Prison Notebooks of Antonio Gramsci*. Ed. and trans. Quintin Hoare and Geoffrey Nowell Smith. New York: International Publishers, 1971.
————. *Il materialismo storico e la filosofia di Benedetto Croce*. Turin: Einaudi, 1972.
Habermas, Jürgen. "Some Conditions for Revolutionizing Late Capitalist Societies (1968)." *Canadian Journal of Political and Social Theory* 7 (Winter/Spring 1983): 32–42.
Haight, Roger. *An Alternative Vision: An Interpretation of Liberation Theology*. New York: Paulist Press, 1985.
Hanke, Lewis. *The Imperial City of Potosí*. The Hague: Nijhoff, 1956.
"Instruction on Certain Aspects of the 'Theology of Liberation' from the Congregation for the Doctrine of the Faith." *Origins* 14 (September 13, 1984): pp. 1, 195–204.
"Instruction on Christian Freedom and Liberation from the Congregation for the Doctrine of the Faith." *Origins* 15 (April 17, 1986): pp. 713, 715–728.
Klaiber, Jeffrey. *Religión y revolución en el Perú 1824–1976*. Lima: Universidad del Pacífico, 1980.
Kudó, Tokihiro. *Hacia una cultura nacional popular*. Lima: Centro de Estudios y Promoción del Desarrollo, 1982.
————. *Práctica religiosa y proyecto histórico: estudio sobre la religiosidad popular en dos barrios de Lima*. Lima: Centro de Estudios y Publicaciones, 1980.
Liss, Sheldon. *Marxist Thought in Latin America*. Berkeley: University of California Press, 1984.
Lowenthal, Abraham F., ed. *The Peruvian Experiment: Continuity and Change under Military Rule*. Princeton: Princeton University Press, 1975.
Mallon, Florencia E. "Murder in the Andes: Patrons, Clients, and the Impact of Foreign Capital, 1860–1922." *Radical History Review* 27: 79–98.
Mann, Michael. "The Social Cohesion of Liberal Democracy." *American Sociological Review* 35 (June 1970): 423–439.
Manuel, Frank E., and Fritzie P. Manuel. *Utopian Thought in the Western World*. Cambridge, Mass.: Belknap Press of Harvard University Press, 1979.
Manzanera, Miguel. *Teología, salvación y liberación en la obra de Gustavo Gutiérrez*. Bilbao: Universidad de Deusto, 1978.
Mariátegui, José María. *Seven Interpretive Essays on Peruvian Reality*. Trans. Marjory Urquidi. Austin: University of Texas Press, 1971.
Metz, Johann Baptist. *Faith in History and Society: Towards a Practical Fundamental Theology*. New York: Seabury, 1980.

136 *Bibliography*

Monast, Jacques. *On les croyait chrétiens: les aymaras.* Paris: Les Editions du Cerf, 1969.
Portes, Alejandro, and John Walton. *Labor, Class and the International System.* New York: Academic Press, 1981.
Sahlins, Martin. *Culture and Practical Reason.* Chicago: University of Chicago Press, 1976.
Schillebeeckx, Edward. *Christ: The Experience of Jesus as Lord.* Trans. John Bowden. New York: Crossroad, 1981.
Segundo, Juan Luis. *The Liberation of Theology.* Trans. John Drury. Maryknoll, N.Y.: Orbis Books, 1984.
Taussig, Michael T. *The Devil and Commodity Fetishism in South America.* Chapel Hill: The University of North Carolina Press, 1980.
Tejada, David. "América Latina: la deuda inmanejable." *Quehacer* 30 (August 1984): pp. 52–61.
Thompson, E.. *The Poverty of Theory and Other Essays.* New York: Monthly Review Press, 1978.
Thompson, John B. "Ideology and the Critique of Domination I." *Canadian Journal of Political and Social Theory* 7 (Winter/Spring 1983): 163–183.
Touraine, Alain. *The Self-Production of Society.* Trans. Derek Coltman. Chicago: University of Chicago Press, 1977.
Turner, Victor. *Dramas, Fields and Metaphors: Symbolic Action and Human Society.* Ithaca: Cornell University Press, 1974.
Vidales, Raúl, and Tokihiro Kudó. *Práctica religiosa y proyecto histórico: hipótesis para un estudio de la religiosidad popular en América Latina.* Lima: Centro de Estudios y Publicaciones, 1975.
Williams, Raymond. *Marxism and Literature.* Oxford: Oxford University Press, 1977.
Willis, Paul E. *Learning to Labour: How Working Class Kids Get Working Class Jobs.* Westmead, Farnborough, Hampshire: Giwer Publishing, Co., 1980.

Secondary Works

Bloch, Ernst. *Man on His Own: Essays in the Philosophy of Religion.* Trans. E. B. Ashton. New York: Herder & Herder, 1970.
———. *A Philosophy of the Future.* Trans. John Cumming. New York: Herder & Herder, 1979.
Bourdieu, Pierre. *Outline of a Theory of Practice.* Trans. Richard Nice. Cambridge: Cambridge University Press, 1977.
Comisión episcopal de acción social. *La justicia en el mundo.* Documento del episcopado peruano para el sínodo. Lima, 1969.
Cormie, Lee. "Society, History, Meaning: Perspectives from the Social Sciences." *The Catholic Theological Society of America: Proceedings of the Thirty-Fourth Annual Convention* 34 (June 13–16, 1979): 31–47.
Correa, Marcial Rubio. "Las Fuerzas Armadas, la política y la doctrina de la contrainsurgencia." *Quehacer* 31 (October 1984): pp. 36–67.
Countryman, Edward, and Susan Deans. "Independence and Revolution in the Americas: A Project for Comparative Study." *Radical History Review* 27 (1985): 144–173.

Documento de la Conferencia Episcopal Peruana sobre la teología de la liberación. *Páginas* Especial — Documentos 65–66 (November–December 1984).

Favre, Henri. "Perú: Sendero Luminoso y horizontes oscuros." *Quehacer* 31 (October 1984): pp. 25–35.

"García's Peru: One Last Chance." *NACLA: Report on the Americas* 20 (June 1986): 13–47.

Giddens, Anthony. "Four Theses on Ideology." *Canadian Journal of Political and Social Theory* 7 (Winter/Spring 1983): 18–21.

Hirst, Paul. "Ideology, Culture and Personality." *Canadian Journal of Political and Social Theory* 7 (Winter/Spring 1983): 118–130.

Hudson, Wayne. "Ernst Bloch: 'Ideology' and Postmodern Social Theory." *Canadian Journal of Political and Social Theory* 7 (Winter/Spring 1983): 131–145.

Iguiñiz, Javier E. *Crisis y fluctuaciones en la economía peruana 1950–1983.* Lima: Tarea, 1985.

Kudó, Tokihiro, and Cecilia Tovar. *La crítica de la religión: ensayo sobre la conciencia social según Marx.* Lima: Centro de Estudios y Publicaciones, 1982.

Levine, Daniel H. "Religion and Politics: Drawing Lines, Understanding Change." *Latin American Research Review* 20 (1985): 185–201.

Lukes, Steven. *Power: A Radical View.* London: McMillan Press, 1981.

Maduro, Otto. "Marxist Analysis and the Sociology of Religion." *Social Compass* 22 (1975): 305–322.

———. *Religion and Social Conflicts.* Trans. Robert R. Barr. Maryknoll, N.Y.: Orbis Books, 1982.

Mannheim, Karl. *Ideology and Utopia: An Introduction to the Sociology of Knowledge.* Trans. Louis Wirth and Edward Shils. New York: Harcourt, Brace & World, 1936.

Marcos, Juan Manuel. "La tenura pensativa de José María Arguedas." *Revista Iberoamericana* No. 127 (April–June 1984): 445–457.

Márkus, György. "Concepts of Ideology in Marx." *Canadian Journal of Political and Social Theory* 7 (Winter/Spring 1983): 84–103.

Matos Mar, José. *Desborde popular y crisis del Estado: el nuevo rostro del Perú en la década de 1980.* Perú Problema series, no. 21. Lima: Instituto de Estudios Peruanos, 1985.

McLellan, David. *Marxism after Marx: An Introduction.* New York: Harper & Row, 1979.

Moreno, César Fernandez. "José María Arguedas en el clivaje de dos culturas." *Revista Iberoamericana* 122 (January–March 1983): 67–82.

Nash, June, Juan Corradi, and Hobart Spalding, Jr., eds. *Ideology and Social Change in Latin America.* New York: Gordon and Breach, 1977.

Nesti, Arnaldo. "Gramsci et la religion populaire." *Social Compass* 22 (1975): 343–354.

Pantigoso, Edgardo J. *La rebelión contra el indigenismo y la afirmación del pueblo en el mundo de José María Arguedas.* Lima: Editorial Juan Mejía Baca, 1981.

Puebla and Beyond. Ed. John Eagleson and Philip Scharper. Maryknoll, N.Y.: Orbis Books, 1979.

Rostow, W. W. *The Stages of Economic Growth, A Non-Communist Manifesto.* Cambridge: Cambridge University Press, 1962.

Rowe, William. *Mito e ideología en la obra de José María Arguedas.* Lima: Instituto Nacional de Cultura, 1979.

Rudé, George. *Ideology and Popular Protest.* New York: Pantheon Books, 1980.

Salinas, Maximiliano, and Diego Irarrázaval. *Hacia una teología de los pobres.* Lima: Centro de Estudios y Publicaciones, 1980.

Scott, Jim. *Weapons of the Weak: Everyday Forms of Peasant Resistance.* New Haven: Yale University Press, 1985.

Segundo, Juan Luis. *Faith and Ideologies.* Trans. John Drury. Maryknoll, N.Y.: Orbis Books, 1984.

Sobrino, Jon. *Christology at the Crossroads: A Latin American Approach.* Trans. John Drury. Maryknoll, N.Y.: Orbis Books, 1978.

Stern, Steve J. "The Struggle for Solidarity: Class, Culture, and Community in Highland Indian America." *Radical History Review* 27: 21–48.

Vallier, Ivan. *Catholicism, Social Control, and Modernization in Latin America.* Englewood Cliffs, N.J.: Prentice Hall, 1970.

Index